MW01658548

What people are

"It takes a special person to take in a child that's not your own. My grandmother and grandfather raised me, and I gave them all kinds of trouble. My grandfather was my grandmother's second husband and I always considered us a family… even when I burned down half of the garage. The families in this book are an inspiration to anyone who wants to adopt. They'll tell it like it is. Thank God for these families, and people like my grandparents. Christine Devine's time on TV on this makes *Finding a Forever Family* worth reading."

George Lopez, Comedian
Star, *The George Lopez Show*

"Celebrities who adopt kids always make headlines. Christine has written a book about hundreds of thousands of other kids, who are just as worthy of adoption but have gone unnoticed. Christine has done more than her share to change that, using the power of television to inform and inspire. She's now expanding her work beyond Los Angeles in her book, *Finding a Forever Family*, that will inspire everyone who reads it."

Harvey Levin
Executive Producer, Host TMZ

"God sent an angel to us and her name is Christine Devine. The dedication she has for children through not only her journey, but the great work of Wednesday's Child, is heaven sent! I know firsthand the need to be a voice for children less fortunate, and it's a lifetime commitment. After getting to know Christine, I realized not only is she an angel, but a great friend!"

Sheila E.
Philanthropist, entertainer and queen of percussion

"It has been really great to host kids from foster care out at Dodger Stadium. Every kid needs to know they are important. I teach my players to make a difference and it has been an honor to do our part for adoption. This book remembers a great kid who was on his way to becoming a young leader. He was proof adoption can change a life."

Tommy Lasorda
Los Angeles Dodgers

"*Finding a Forever Family* brings a message of hope for our young who are seeking a new life to be loved and the families who will provide those needs. A messenger is needed in these difficult times and it's Christine Devine. The families in this nation who provide a home and a proper place for the growth of a child also build the institution of a greater America."

Carol Channing, Comedienne
Author, *Just Lucky I Guess*

"*Finding a Forever Family* is real and deep as it does not sugar-coat the realities of loving wounded children from the foster care system. Our journeys make us who we are. Christine's reality gives her a true sense of adoption. ONLY Christine can tell this story as she has lived it personally and professionally! The entire experience is what makes her who she is today."

Dr. Pat Allen, Marriage/Family Therapist
Best-selling author of *Getting To I Do*; *The Truth About Men*

"Finding happiness can be difficult for children in the world of foster care. Adoptive parents can be a big step in helping them have a dream, and I'm glad to see so many businesses playing a role in giving these children a day to remember. Christine's book, *Finding a Forever Family*, offers a unique perspective to the world of adoption and foster care."

Tony Hsieh, CEO of Zappos.com, Inc.
#1 New York Times bestselling author of *Delivering Happiness*

"*Finding a Forever Family* is a must read book for anyone who has ever thought of adopting a child. You will laugh and you will cry as you read this touching memoir. Told with brutal honestly of the realities of adopting out of the foster care system, Devine shares the highs and lows from the adoptive kids and parents' perspective. Read on and see if there's a foster child out there awaiting your arrival as their "forever family."

Victorya Rogers, Life Coach
Author, *Finding a Man Worth Keeping*

"As someone who has worked with foster children, I have seen firsthand the faces of the children who so desperately want the love and support of a permanent home. Christine's segments have helped so many of these kids realize their dream."

Shaun Robinson, Co-anchor, *Access Hollywood*
Author, *Exactly As I Am*
Past spokesperson for the L.A. County Share Your Heart, Share Your Home Program

"Christine Devine is a stalwart advocate for children in need. Her segment continues to help children find homes and draws attention to the critical issue of adoption."

US Senator Dianne Feinstein- California
nominated Christine for Congressional award

"It has been my experience that when people set out to change a life through adoption, the life that ends up most changed is their own. Because of Christine, over 500 children have the love and support of a forever family. We were proud to honor her for this and for the hundreds more that have yet to be touched by her work. Like her fellow Angels in Adoption, Christine's extraordinary journey began with a single step forward—saying 'count me in.'"

Kathleen Strottman, Executive Director
Congressional Coalition on Adoption Institute

"In a world full of vain, vacuous celebrities, Christine has skillfully used her fame and position in the media to help foster children find permanent, loving homes. Many of these children have suffered severe abuse and been bounced from one placement to another for years, crushing any sense of security or trust they might have had. Christine, through her work with Wednesday's Child, has helped them to finally find a secure, loving, safe place in this world."

Alison Arngrim, "Nellie" on *Little House on the Prairie*
New York Times Best Selling author of
Confessions of A Prairie Bitch
Board Member of the National Association to
PROTECT Children (PROTECT.org)

"Christine Devine is among the many heroes of the foster care system. Through her enduring work on Wednesday's Child over the past fifteen years, hundreds of children in Los Angeles County have been adopted and provided safety, and permanence, which are the two most critical elements in building a solid foundation for any child to have a bright future."

Dr. Charles J. Sophy, FACN
Medical Director Los Angeles County Department of
Child and Family Services
Author, *Side by Side: The Revolutionary Mother-Daughter*
Program for Conflict-Free Communication

"Some very special foster children need a little extra help in finding just the right person, the right family to call their very own, 'forever family.' That's when Christine Devine and her Wednesday's Child program step up, step in and create a miracle. A family who didn't even plan on adopting suddenly finds themselves falling in love with a child that they first saw on a television program; all because of a special woman, a wonderful program and the loving connections that come from creating a family. Thank you Christine Devine and Wednesday's Child, for making the world a better place, one child and one family at a time."

Trish Ploehn
Former Director Los Angeles County Department of
Children and Family Services

"Those of us in the broadcast profession understand the power of television… but few of us put it to good use like Christine Devine. Christine's work with Wednesday's Child has been nothing short of remarkable. Despite her demanding schedule, she goes out of her way to make a personal connection with each of these kids. I believe that connection is what transcends the medium of television and inspires viewers to bring these children into their lives. Christine Devine is synonymous with Wednesday's Child in the Greater Los Angeles area—and we are a more connected community because of it."

Wendy Burch, Founder
The Good News Foundation

"You must read this book if you are looking to adopt. You'll see the real world of adoption through the eyes of these families. It is a candid look that can only be told by someone who's walked this walk, Christine Devine. Christine is a humanitarian in every sense of the word. Every child in foster care is reflected in *Finding a Forever Family*."

Lilly Fallah Lawrence, Humanitarian
Honored with the "Defender of the First Amendment"
Award, George Washington University

"This fabulous book demonstrates how every single one of us has the ability to impact and change the life of a foster child, by showering them with support and love, regardless of whether or not we are able to adopt. I strongly encourage you to buy this book in bulk and give copies to everyone you know that cares about America's lost children!"

Stacia Oemig, Founder
Project Nightlight

"Too many children from foster care grow up with no place to turn, no guidance, and no leadership, leaving them out on our streets. Christine and Wednesday's Child are working to turn the tide for children who end up in the system... through no fault of their own."

Sheriff Leroy D. Baca
Los Angeles County Sheriff's Department

"One of the comments that I get from the kids of the WC TV shoots is that they felt like a movie star for the day! All of the children have LOVED doing something new and exciting like ice skating or going to a Dodgers game with Christine. They have loved being treated like a VIP and most have remarked on the way home that Christine is the first person (besides me) who has asked them how they really feel about adoption and foster care. The taping of the children has made them seem much more than just their history."

Kim Felder, Recruiter
Wendy's Wonderful Kids, LA County Kinship Center

"I'd always wanted to be a police officer so I was thrilled when Christine called for me to host a teen with the same dream. I know that same look in her eyes when she arrived at the police station for her 'Dream Day.' I too remember my first ride in a police car. Don't just make a difference in a child's life, Be the difference. "

Cristina Coria, Retired Police Officer
CBS *Survivor—Cook Islands*, Contestant

"Success isn't success unless you are able to give back. I've loved doing 'Dream Days' for Christine's children in foster care. To make a young lady look and feel beautiful is an easy job. To make them feel safe and loved is another. Congratulations to every person who ever adopts. YOUR success is unmatched."

Carol Shaw, Celebrity Makeup Artist
Creator of LORAC Cosmetics

"Mrs. Devine, I wanted to say that I am very happy that you help to get me adopted. Because my Parents really take good care of us, they also have made sure that I've had a roof over my head. And have good clean clothes to wear and food to always eat. And I no longer have to go from one home to another. I really like it here and I want to stay here, also that's why I am happy that I got adopted. Thank you Wednesday Child."

Brooklyn Moreland Williams
Adoptee

"We also would like to thank Wednesday's Child for the opportunity given to us as a family to be a part of such a great endeavor, though we only have a small part to play in a puzzle so large. We feel that having Brooklyn in our home has made a great impact on the family and community in which he now resides. Brooklyn is a very happy and outgoing child and is deserving of all the good coming to him. Again, we thank you for enlarging our hearts."

Kermit and Shelley Williams
Adoptive Parents

"I first saw Michelle on the Fox News segment entitled Wednesday's Child. She was on the pier in Santa Monica with Christine doing an interview at seven and a half years old. She appeared so shy and timid, yet I could see that she was blossoming in Christine's presence. Apparently there was a lot of life bubbling under that shy appearance. Eleven years later and I've seen her zest for life. Michelle is a beautiful, vibrant young woman. She graduated recently and has enlisted in the Army. I am so proud of her and her accomplishments in life."

Frances Abbott
Adoptive parent

"Clark is without question the best! He and his sister Julia bring so much joy not only to our lives but to everyone they meet. They're truly special individuals destined for big things. Gil and I are so blessed to be their parents."

Kelly
Adoptive Parent

“I wanted to be a father and didn’t really think I was doing anything out of the ordinary, but all the folks behind Wednesday’s Child really made me feel special, almost like a celebrity, which was a pleasant surprise. When we first saw the segment on Emilio and Alex on the Wednesday’s Child website, we played it over and over again, studying their every word and move! ”

Ted Persky
Adoptive Parent

“From year to year there are 35-50,000 foster children without a voice in Los Angeles... Christine Devine is the angel and voice for at-risk orphans and we Angelenos are grateful she is.”

Gavin Glynn
Adoptive Parent

FINDING A FOREVER **FAMILY**

By
Christine Devine

with
Allison Bottke

IPG

Intermedia Publishing Group

Finding a Forever Family

Published by:
Intermedia Publishing Group, Inc.
P.O. Box 2825
Peoria, Arizona 85380
intermediapub.com

ISBN 978-1-935906-42-1

The official title of the program referenced in this book is; Freddie Mac Foundation's Wednesday's Child, and may be referred to in *Finding a Forever Family* as Wednesday's Child or WC.

For privacy reasons, some names and locations in *Finding a Forever Family* have been changed.

Most family photos by Will Wong

Cover photo by Michael Herbach

WWW.MHPHOTOGRAPHY.COM
Michael Herbach Photography (310) 640-9846

Interior photos by Will Wong, Jody Domingue Studios and Michael Herbach

JODY DOMINGUE STUDIOS
WWW.JODYDOMINGUE.COM

Website design by the lab+
thelabdesign.com

CONTENTS

PART THREE—Appendices

DEDICATION

To Skylar Emma

Your eyes light up the room.

May every child know such innocence.

On the Set

INTRODUCTION

My Inspiration

Ask not what your country... er, I mean company... ask not what your company can do for you, but what you can do for your company. It was a philosophy I lived by and I was every bit the yes man... I mean woman. I wanted very much to please; it pained me to ever let anyone down. So, when my company, my television station, asked me to cover an adoption segment, of course I said yes. I was a young reporter/anchor at a Los Angeles news station and I was now assigned to "Sunday's Child."

It was a weekly segment that had aired on another channel, the reporter had retired and we picked it up. Sunday's Child was a story on the 10 p.m. news that profiled children in foster care waiting to be adopted. I wasn't the first to do it. I'm not the last. Perhaps not even the best. I was, however, an unlikely advocate.

I loved my boss, News Director, Jose Rios, and did not want to disappoint. I agreed to the assignment, put on my professional hat and suited up for the job. Literally, in fact, as I'd leave my anchor attire at home and don what one colleague called "costumes." If we were shooting at Pa's Pumpkin Patch I wore my blue-jean overalls. If we were at a Lakers practice with Kobe Bryant I was in my basketball sweats. If we were on the runway for L.A. Fashion week I was a fashionista and red-carpet ready. Wherever we went I dressed the part. Even played the part. We even went Hollywood.

In L.A. there is no shortage of celebs and the kids got to pose for pictures with rock star Gene Simmons of KISS, singer Jessica Simpson, and actress Emma Roberts.

Every bit the professional... or make that the scared young reporter... I did my job to the best of my abilities. I shot my stories, logged the tape, wrote the script, got them into edit, and on air. Little did viewers (or barely anyone for that matter) know the turmoil that brewed inside my heart and head.

You see, while I hoped adoption would work for others, and always loved the adorable little children, the truth was that I wasn't thoroughly convinced adoption worked. The battle that waged in my mind and memory concerned my own family's adoption. A perfect picture had been tainted by unrest within my own household, and it was a burden I'd shouldered since I was ten years old. We had struggled so much after my parents welcomed a boy from foster care into our home. Mike was only eight when he was adopted, yet his cute little dimpled face couldn't hide the heartbreak inside. My mom, dad, and little sister, Danielle all weathered the storms in our own ways. The years were peppered with chaos, and it was a festering personal wound that I seldom discussed with anyone and wrestled with often as this assignment wore on.

I swore I'd never adopt. I assumed God would understand and forgive. We'd had too much turmoil, too much worry. It was an unwritten pact, one that needed no explanation. So when asked to take on an adoption segment you might imagine my inner expression. *You're kidding me, right? Surely, God must be playing a cruel joke.*

On the outside I smiled brightly and went to work. After all, who was I to judge? I was certain others had a rewarding experience. I'd always imagined adoption meant "a happy ending" for someone, somewhere. If a person wanted to adopt, my theory was "go for it." My assignment was to showcase children waiting for a "Forever Family." No problem. Easily done and without bias. But it would stay professional, and never personal.

That was until Sunday's Child became Wednesday's Child... and I met Jared.

PART ONE

Alicia interviewed on her adoption day

Chapter 1

Wednesday's Child

No, I did not invent Wednesday's Child. That's a question I'm often asked, as I've been on the news here in Los Angeles for twenty years as the KTTV Fox 11 10 p.m. anchor every Monday through Friday. Wednesday's Child is a known name in this large and diverse city, and for many of our viewers a warm moment in the sea of negative news. I'm always thrilled when people see me on the streets, point their finger and say knowingly, "Wednesday's Child. I love Wednesday's Child!"

Truth is, I love it too! No longer the "scared rookie reporter," I've been around the block a time or two since those early days.

It took about eight years before the segment started finding a comfortable place in people's homes and hearts. Now, after fifteen years on-air, it's a signature segment on our newscast and I am blessed to be the face of it. So often people congratulate me, not aware that there is a whole team behind it. I lovingly call them TEAM WC.

So many have said, "you do so much for the kids." It is welcome praise, but what most folks never know is how much the children have done for me. I consider each and every one of them a divine gift (no pun intended).

"Devine... is that your real last name?"

It's a question I've gotten my entire career life. People often think it is a stage name made up to sound smooth and glamorous for my TV news anchor job. In reality, it's my adopted last name. I was born Christine Yara Lucas.

The story of my adoption is not to be confused with those I cover on Wednesday's Child, where my assignment is to profile children in foster care "waiting" to be adopted. I had never been in foster care, was never removed from my birth family. I was born in upstate New York to a single mother. She married Jack Duane Devine when I was three years old. He legally adopted me and my last name became his. It became ours. We were a family and I was now Christine Yara Devine.

I never noticed I was minus my birth father as I was too young and he was never in the picture. I'd never met him, nor seen a photo, nor was he discussed. As my grandparents played an important role, I was never minus the love, safety and permanency of a forever home and Jack Devine was "dad." I did however wonder why my last name by birth was Lucas and who this mystery man I referred to as "my birth father" was. I wondered too why, with my brown skin and curly hair, I didn't look like anyone else in my anglo family. Not knowing a birth parent was something with which I felt a kinship with many of the children on Wednesday's Child.

Wednesday's Child is a way to announce to the world that there are children waiting to be adopted. Children in the United States of America. Children in foster care in need of loving, safe, permanent homes. Reserved for the cases considered "hardest to place"... older children, large sibling groups, and children with severe special needs, our children are often overlooked for the more sought after babies. The children we profile are at-risk kids, desperate for love, yet caught up in a system doing its best with a crisis that can be cruel and unforgiving.

I call some of our kids from Wednesday's Child, "Adoption Ambassadors," and although I am "officially" the reporter, I've grown to refer to myself "unofficially" as their Greatest Cheerleader. GO TEAM WC!

But as I said earlier, I wasn't always chanting this cheer.

It Started on a Sunday

Sunday's Child was the original name of our segment when we launched in 1994 and when it aired previously on another channel. It changed to Wednesday's Child in 2000 when the national Freddie Mac Foundation came calling.

Still, at that time I was all business. I did the job without complaint yet also without personal passion. A stoic resilience you might say. Knowing the end result, here's the irony. This is not ever an issue I wanted to tackle. It wasn't my "cause celeb." Sure, I could do the job, but no way was this personal. I didn't want it to get personal. I buried the wounds of my own family chapter deep down inside, fearing that any shred of transparent truthfulness would have only rendered me useless.

At first, the extra fun in the assignment was that it was a chance to get out of the office. People don't realize that anchoring is an office job. You only get out if you are reporting or on an interview. I grew to love all of the different shoot locations and nearby cities. Rocky Mountain Chocolate Factory in Belmont Shore near Long Beach. Ice Skating at Pershing Square downtown. Color Me Mine in Valencia. With the Anaheim Ducks hockey team and Angels baseball team in Orange County. Chefs Inc. in West L.A. Platinum Publicity's gift suites in Hollywood. Wednesday's Child was a chance to see more of L.A. A chance to meet new people.

I would shoot the weekly segment, log the tape, and write the story with only the facts given in the interviews with the children and social workers. I forged ahead with one goal in mind. To do my job. To profile children in foster care waiting to be adopted. No more, no less. I played the role of the neutral, unbiased journalist. The calm, cool, collected, non-phased career gal.

But that didn't last long, because no matter how hard I tried, I wasn't cool, calm and collected. When it came to kids in crisis I wasn't a neutral, unbiased journalist. I take no position on policy or on L.A. County's perspective on foster care and adoption, I do, however, have a mama bear fight in me when it comes to these innocent kids in the system through no fault of their own. A kid is just a kid, and I aim to treat all with respect, with no disrespect to their past or to their birth parents. From time to time I have the opportunity to meet birth parents, and I've come to see that they often carry their own pain in this difficult journey.

Memories of Mike

In spite of my professional posture, I was a mess of emotions during the early years of Wednesday's Child. Over the years painful feelings surfaced, issues I never knew I had. I started asking questions not yet knowing I was trying to answer my own internal issues. At times I was even angry. Often I had doubts. On rare occasions I wanted little part of it.

The truth was, my own parents had adopted and fostered older children, and for us, it wasn't "happily-ever-after." It was a mixed bag. Because, while my adopted brother caused great disappointment, pain and turmoil, my foster sister, Bao Tran (Terissa) Nguyen, remains among the best things to happen to me. While my adopted brother left me questioning if I would ever recommend adoption, my foster sister had me screaming "Yes!"

While my adopted brother never seemed to bond with my father, my foster brother became dad's beloved sidekick and golfing buddy. While my adopted brother's life ended tragically, the foster kids my parents took in are all out on their own. All attended college. All moved to other states. Two are married. One is a Navy doctor.

I was conflicted at worst, confused at best.

The story of my adopted brother is sadly nothing unusual for the foster care system. He was eight when we met. I was ten years old, Danielle was five. It's a heartbreaking story.

Mike was born in jail. His mother was fifteen and addicted to heroin. He'd lived with his grandmother until he was five years old when she decided she could no longer keep him. Mike remembered the day well. "I was sitting on the swing set. I was crying." That was the day the social worker came to get him. A vision of that sad little boy is etched in my mind and always haunted me.

Mike's life story with my family is one that might scare away most any unsuspecting prospective parent. To understand kids in foster care you must understand that all come from a family in trauma. That is why they are in foster care.

Despite my parents offering him a happy home, Mike made a lot of devastating if not just plain stupid choices that changed his life and the lives of those around him. He was introduced to drugs by a neighbor at eleven years old and would continue to dance with the devil. My mom believes he self-medicated. Just tuned out. Found peace in drugs. Wherever we went, wherever we moved, Mike found the saying "birds of a feather..." to be true. He'd always find the kids who used drugs. None were in the system; none were foster or adopted kids. To this day I wonder if the pain of a parent is different if the child is their own by birth. Or do they share a commonality?

During Mike's teen years we were familiar with the police. As he grew up he went from juvenile hall to freedom to prison to freedom to prison and on and on. He died of a cocaine overdose at thirty-three. It was a constant chaos that left me traumatized. Danielle seems to be less scarred and left with less emotion and question.

"He wasted his life, it's just sad," she says.

What happened to that scrumptious eight-year-old boy? Perhaps he buried his wounds in drug abuse. Perhaps there was a genetic addiction. Perhaps he was just always in the wrong place at the wrong time. I was hard pressed to believe others when they would say things like "perhaps the tragedy of his life played out exactly as it was meant to, a journey designed for some higher purpose."

It's hard to believe the latter, especially when we lose someone we cared for and actually liked. I really liked Mike. The Mike I knew was gentle and kind of funny. We had a bond.

The reality of the Mike experience is that it helped make me who I am, the good and the bad. Mike taught me sympathy for those suffering, a fear of illegal drug use, a passion for going forward in spite of life challenges, and a will to never stop the fight for those less fortunate. Through Mike I learned there was a story behind everyone.

But was it a story I would ever tell?

When my boss asked me to take on this new television segment in 1995 to find "Forever Families" for children in foster care, all I could think of was Mike.

I knew I could do the job, but I thought that is all it would be—a job.

How wrong I was.

On the Job

At the news station—on studio turf—I was the serious news anchor. Business suit and all, striving for credibility. In the field it was a different story. I was a different girl. You might say I literally let my hair down. The kid-friendly segment meant for kid-friendly locations. Magic Mountain meant roller coaster rides. If we went to a Dodgers game I'd throw on my navy blue Dodgers baseball cap. If shooting with the L.A. Galaxy I'd wear my team soccer jersey with "Devine" on the back. Blue jeans and tennis shoes were a regular on a shoot day and it was often obvious when I arrived at the office that it was a Wednesday's Child shoot day. I became a kid all over again. When interviewing the children, for them, I wasn't just another adult in a suit. We had fun! I began to see the world through the eyes of some amazing children, and it began to change my life.

What it also did was to soften my serious image and show a personality not seen when reading the nightly news back then. Seems the public started viewing me as a cheerleader for children in foster care. And who wouldn't want to come along? We went bike riding at the beach, flew kites along the sea shore, went shopping for trendy jeans, went to the circus, Disney on Ice, made pizza, frosted cupcakes, dipped chocolate strawberries, went to the aquarium, walked red carpets, and posed for pictures. We met all the famous athletes (Lakers, Clippers, Dodgers, Angels, Kings, Sparks). On one shoot Kobe Bryant even ripped the Nikes off his feet and gave them to our kid! All this for our TV profiles on children in foster care.

The attention it brought began to scare me. It was all so surprising, a bit confusing, a tad overwhelming, a lot unexpected, and at times even frightening.

Wednesday's Child started becoming a fan favorite. People would toss out words like "hero" and "angel." I began to get viewer e-mail and Facebook fan mail. Certainly these kind, well meaning viewers couldn't be referring to me? I was just doing my job.

There was no doubt the children were just that, beautiful little children. And although I do take credit for putting together some warm and wonderful stories, I saw nothing heroic about it. Heroes were people of great giving and sacrifice. Angels were of another breed. I come from a family of middle class philanthropists. Educators, foreign aid workers, community volunteers. My standards were set high and I in no means could match that of my mother. In her early twenties, she left America for Brazil. For a few years, she lived and worked in the slums, the favelas. Mom would tell stories of traveling to rural villages to give immunizations to native people. She'd share her shower with the families living on the hilltop. She'd cart a movie projector up the hills and broadcast old classics on a sheet. Mom said she never felt unsafe and the neighbor families would keep a watch on *the American* as she walked home alone at night. My work, in my mind, paled in comparison. She'd lived in the poorest of conditions. I lived in Hollywood. I worked on TV. Hardly worth accolades in my estimation, especially knowing I was only doing my job.

> "Success isn't success unless you are able to give back. I've loved doing "Dream Days" for Christine's children in foster care. To make a young lady look and feel beautiful is an easy job. To make them feel safe and loved is another. Congratulations to every person who ever adopts. YOUR success is unmatched."
>
> Carol Shaw, Celebrity Makeup Artist and Creator of LORAC Cosmetics

I had yet to comprehend that we all have something to offer in our own unique way. I had yet to understand that perhaps we are all where we are for some divine plan. My mentor, Attorney Emily Card, once asked me to write what I would want on my epitaph. I was in my mid-twenties so I wasn't quite sure. I came up with "She Made a Difference." I had yet to see that come true. My "Wednesday's Child Ambassadors" had yet to reveal themselves. TEAM WC was not yet born.

At the time questions still hovered. *Why would someone want to adopt? Were prospective parents prepped properly? Would the children respond to their new families? Could these kids overcome their jarring pasts? Did Wednesday's Child really work?*

Answers to those questions would come over time as I began to see that finding a forever family wasn't something reserved just for our WC kids.

Freddie Mac Foundation C.E.O. Ralph Boyd on National Adoption Day

Chapter 2

How it All Begins

To know the story of Jared, to know his legacy, you must first know the beginning. How it starts—how kids end up in "the system," in foster care, and eventually, on Wednesday's Child. How it all begins.

WC (as I'll largely call it from now on), is a program sponsored by the Freddie Mac Foundation. We were among five cities selected to join this amazing commitment, along with D.C., Atlanta, Philadelphia, and New York. That's when we went from Sunday's Child to Wednesday's Child. The profile segments didn't change, just the title and we were thrilled to be a part of a more polished national program.

The Freddie Mac Foundation was created in 1991, and is at the heart of Freddie Mac's philanthropy. The Foundation is a not-for-profit corporation that is sustained through its own charitable endowment.

The Foundation has made this issue their cause. As a major corporate funder in the Washington, D.C. region, Freddie Mac and the Foundation have invested more than $348 million to create stable homes and communities.

Some of their special programs include:

> The Freddie Mac Foundation Heart Gallery: a photo exhibit of children in foster care waiting to be adopted.

The Freddie Mac Foundation Adoption Expo: an annual event that provides a wealth of information on adoption for the community.

National Adoption Day: Over the years, more than 20,000 foster care adoptions have been finalized on National Adoption Day. (Started in Los Angeles by Judge Michael Nash, fellow Angels in Adoption honoree.)

Being able to partner with the Freddie Mac Foundation was a tremendous opportunity—not only for us—but for the kids in our community. Foundation sponsorship meant funding, which also meant new rules and regulations. We had to be ultra-accountable. We had to take our program to a new level—on many levels.

It also meant our continued collaboration with the Los Angeles County Department of Children and Family Services (DCFS). WC is one of many recruitment efforts DCFS uses to find permanent families for children in the foster care system. Permanent families, not foster families. "Forever Families"—people wanting to adopt. WC would not exist as we know it if not for this critical partnership. While we work in tandem to achieve one ultimate goal, you might say Wednesday's Child is the cart to the DCFS horse, not the reverse.

> "We're proud of our work since 1991 to help children and families in need. By investing in, and partnering with non-profits that serve our community, we've been able to make life better for children and families."
>
> Ralph F. Boyd, Jr.
> Executive Vice President,
> Freddie Mac and President and CEO,
> Freddie Mac Foundation

Program Coordinator, Will Wong, explains their role.

It Starts Here

The Los Angeles County Department of Children and Family Services (DCFS) is the largest public child welfare agency in the nation. Given its size and population density, it's also the nation's largest public adoption agency. I'm a Placement and Recruitment Coordinator in the Adoption and Permanency Resources Division of DCFS.

As such, I am in charge of adoption recruitment for the children who have gone through the court process of family reunification unsuccessfully.

Albeit one of several methods, Wednesday's Child is the most intensive form of recruitment due to the use of broadcast media when all other measures to find an adoptive family have proved unfruitful. In many ways, the WC program mirrors the court process. When all methods to reunify a child with their biological family fail, another form of permanency is sought—adoption.

WC is in larger part a DCFS program. The children come from us, we assess the children who appear on the program and take on the continued responsibility of matching, case conferencing, full disclosures and working with the families selected for adoption.

Officially, I'm also the Program Coordinator of the Wednesday's Child program produced in partnership with the Freddie Mac Foundation, FOX 11, and my agency, the Los Angeles County Department of Children and Family Services.

LA DCFS is a little known law enforcement body who investigates allegations of child abuse of various forms. Los Angeles County alone responds to an

> average of 140,000 allegations of abuse and neglect annually.

The number one job of DCFS workers is to protect children from abuse, neglect and abandonment. Not a pretty picture, not a pretty job.

Enter the secondary job. When children are removed from a birth home, the job of DCFS is to find families to foster them.

"While making the primary effort to reunify them with their biological parents, first and foremost we try to place children with relatives under foster care, but that doesn't always work out so we seek to place from our pool of licensed foster parents," said Will.

Foster homes serve as a safe house. They provide food and shelter, take the children to school, make their meals. They are meant to be temporary, although some can last for years and years.

There are two possible scenarios when a child enters foster care. In most cases, it means there is a birth relative working with the county to regain or gain custody. It could be the parent, a grandparent, an aunt, uncle, brother, or sister. Somewhere, there is a birth connection with the hopes of the child returning home.

In other cases, that will never happen, and there is a need for a "new" home.

On rare occasion, there is no birth relative to be found. Some children are true orphans. Whatever the scenario, the fact is many children are left shuffling through the foster care system, often bouncing from home to home. And says Will,

> ...school to school because they are moving from community to community, having to make new friends, new connections and God forbid but they do, having to think about where they want to live and

> with whom. No child should ever have to do this but 'ours' do, our kids have to.

Without an adoptive family, when they turn eighteen they will "emancipate," and simply put this means they are out in the world alone.

"It's a critical time," Will goes on to explain.

> Too often, by the time the children are done with the fantasy that their biological parents or family members will ever get it together, they are faced with the ominous age of adulthood, eighteen, an age where services will be cut off and they'll be left alone on their own to their own devices, and that's when reality hits. I'm alone.
>
> For Wednesday's Child, we are accustomed to getting those cases where time is now even more critical than ever, cases where other methods of adoption recruitment have not yielded results or a teen that had been resistant is finally coming to a place where they want to be adopted and we have less than a year to pull that off.
>
> At WC, we lobby kids who really are running out of time. We intervene for those whose circumstances we know from experience will waste time and operate in tandem with other efforts to produce results. At Wednesday's Child, we hear the cries of kids, read between the lines that they don't want to be alone, and so we give them a really big shot at it… I see us as looking out for the ones who can or will slip through the cracks. We're the ones who pay extra attention and really focus all efforts each week to make that happen for one specific kid or specific sibling set.
>
> We're looking out.

While not all states take on adoption work through their child protective services, many counties in California have, especially Los Angeles. I've asked to Will to give us the official word on this information.

> Our obligation is to expedite permanency for all kids who enter into the system. Firstly, reunifying them with their birth parents or relatives and when that's not possible adoption is the preferred method to achieve permanency. To expedite this process for all kids in the system, all kids are 'remanded' if you will to 'concurrent planning' where while birth parents are working on complying with court orders to get their kids back, we are also working on an alternate plan should the children not reunify, so that no time is wasted should parents fail to reunify and the kids get out of the system into a family, be it their own biological or an adoptive family as quickly as possible. Having a social worker and judge in your life growing up is not what we want for any child or family for that matter.

Wednesday's Child once faced the ugly accusation of protestors. "Wednesday's Child breaks up families. How much are they paying you to steal children?" It broke my heart to hear these words, as I thought we were doing good. It made me realize, however, that I was the face of a matter that involved birth families and an often bitter battle. What some birth families don't seem to understand is that my role as the host of WC comes in after-the-fact. The county is recruiting for adoption with or without me at the point of Wednesday's Child. No, it is not a perfect system. And yes, while I'm largely unaware of the circumstances that led them to this place, I can imagine how painful the situation must be, yet the issue is beyond my control.

Will outlines the process for moving forward.

Reality for Forever Families

The paramount goal is to meet the needs of the children and not the other way around. Children who have a history of abuse and neglect are still healing and can't be expected to meet the needs of the family. Too often this ideal is blurred. This needs to be prefaced, as this is what I see as the primary role played by every social worker in my agency, including myself. To continue to protect the children by getting their needs met first and that means finding or matching the child with the best possible family in order to do that. Once their needs are met and their safety ensured, children can then grow into their forever families.

WC is not simply just watching TV, falling in love and dropping by the shelter to pick up a kid. Just doesn't happen that way. In as much as we want to get kids adopted, it is the social workers who fight their battles in court, intervene in a multitude of circumstances, ready the child for adoption, and ultimately make sure their needs are being met. Sometimes we have to buck the system to make things happen for our kids, and this is perhaps the core of social work.

When an approved family is identified, we have conferences with social workers involved, full disclosure meetings with prospective parents, preparations with the child for the first meeting, monitoring the first meeting, assessing if further visits should happen, monitoring those further visits, helping prospective parents through hurdles in the adjustment and of course, first and foremost the adjustments of the kids. Then the child has to physically live with the prospective parents for at least six months before we even recommend to the court to finalize the adoption, all the while under the watchful eye of social workers who continue to assess and intervene.

Prospective parents need to know there is so much more than just picking up the phone.

Not for Everyone

Some children absolutely don't want to be adopted. We don't ever force them. Wednesday's Child is there for those who want to consider being adopted. We ask a lot from our kids. We ask them to tell their story on TV. To admit they are in foster care. To then have to face kids in school who may see their segment. I applaud their courage. We celebrate their uniqueness! Our goal is for them to know they are important and that someone cares. I love our VIP days because even if a child is never adopted, they will at minimum walk away with a day they will never forget. It's a special child willing to take the chance on love who is the face of Wednesday's Child.

Jared at first took the step slightly reluctantly. He made clear he had a birth aunt who loved him very much. Still he was in foster care. He said he'd go on the program "so other kids would find

> "The stories and happy endings go on and on. All because of a special woman, a wonderful program and the loving connections that come from creating a family. Thank you Christine Devine and Wednesday's Child, for making the world a better place, one child and one family at a time."
>
> Trish Ploehn,
> L.A. County Department of Children and Family Services

a family." Turned out he found one too, and eventually stepped in to the role of one of our first Wednesday's Child advocates, sharing his own story of adoption with personality, passion, and purpose.

One of our teens in foster care at his news shoot

Chapter 3

The Children of Foster Care

"My mom sleeps a lot," he said sadly.

The little boy was in foster care and on an adoption shoot. He seemed to be excited about the day but I'm sure he didn't fully understand. More likely, his mom was on drugs. I understood all too well. Remember, my brother was born in jail. There was the boy whose brother was a gang banger. The teen girl who'd been molested by her father. The boy whose parent was mentally ill, homeless off and on. The twins whose father died. The girl so physically challenged her parents relinquished custody. The brothers who told me their mother took them to a friend's home and never returned. These are some of the faces of foster care. These are the cases the social workers deal with each and every day. These are the children of WC.

Children in foster care are not usually orphans. Yes, I've had cases where the birth parent(s) died. Generally, birth parents are still around, but they've lost custody. The reason being: abuse, abandonment or neglect.

The children of these troubled parents, through no fault of their own, end up in the care of the county or state. Imagine being a child in the middle of all this. Will knows well the details.

> So often, that painful, dysfunctional life seems normal to them.

> In reality, most of the kids we remove from abusive homes don't know that it's abuse until someone like me goes in there and tells them it is. Then, everything that they know, no matter how horrible, unspeakable, albeit 'normal' in their eyes, changes forever.
>
> Of course the kids are angry. We turned their world upside down. Everything they knew that was 'normal' they've internalized and the struggle is accepting happiness and stability when all you've known is chaos as the norm. It's confusing, and while the system and laws set up by society largely protects their physical health, the emotional and psychological impacts are often woefully misunderstood and ignored.
>
> Kids grow up far too fast in the system, having to realize things that kids should not have to realize (that no one should have to realize). The ugly things some adults are capable of, adults (parents) who you were supposed to trust are now revealed as the villains and now, who do you trust? Your attorney, social worker, the judge? You become bitter and jaded, things that aren't supposed to happen to kids.
>
> In the system designed to protect them, it's often a roller coaster ride that is even more confusing as people with their own agendas and personal views sometimes manipulate the law to satisfy their own needs rather than what is needed for the children affected. Although there is progress starting with new laws to protect children, we still have a long way to go from not viewing children as property.

For some children, entering into foster care is devastating. For others, it saves their lives, physically and emotionally.

Keep in mind that most children who ever enter foster care are never on to the next step, adoption. Add to that, almost 50 percent who proceed toward adoption are adopted by a birth relative. Many foster parents go on to adopt too. I love National Adoption Day seeing all the aunts, uncles and grandparents stepping up to save these innocent children. Only a sliver proceed to Wednesday's Child.

Why can't all go with birth relatives? In some cases, birth relatives are no better off. Perhaps they are elderly or there are health issues. Perhaps none can be located by social services.

"Sometimes birth parents are less than forth coming with that information and perhaps dealing with their own shame of not letting their respective families know they're needing help and that their kids are in the system or just simply distrust of the system or anger issues not resolved with their own families," said Will.

An example, we had one woman recognize her brother's children on our adoption segment. She is a law enforcement officer. She called and adopted the whole bunch. In certain cases, children keep contact with birth family with the blessing of their adoptive parents. One little girl brought her brother to our reunion. She was adopted. He lives with a grandparent. In another case an aunt was there every step of the way for her nephew but had no room for him in her home. I loved doing a story on one very special scenario. The adoptive family spends Thanksgiving at the

> "Christine Devine is among the many heroes of the foster care system. Through her enduring work, hundreds of children have been adopted and provided safety, and permanence, which are the two most critical elements in building a solid foundation for any child to have a bright future."
>
> Dr. Charles J. Sophy, FACN
> Author of Side by Side: The Revolutionary Mother-Daughter Program for Conflict-Free Communication

home of their adopted daughter's birth father. He'd been in jail, but life had turned around. Now, they share in life together.

My role is to work with those children who do need adoptive homes. It is a ruling by the courts. Reunification efforts have been severed, and the court has ordered DCFS to proceed with adoption recruitment as Will says, "with full force and effect."

It is no surprise a child might still long for their birth parent. One boy wanted to wrap up a hot dog from our shoot and take it to his birth mom. Another told me of their weekly visits with their parents. Others have a fond childhood memory. Will paints a more specific picture of the birth parents.

> I acknowledge that in spite of dysfunction some did have a genuine love for their kids before their lives went horribly wrong. They did share tender and meaningful moments with their kids. Which is why it's so hard for some kids to let go. We're not asking them to discard it. There's gotta be some real love there. With adoption there's just more people to love you.

If you knew the inside stories they'd break your heart. I rarely did and I vowed to never let it get personal. Then one day, I found I couldn't resist.

A Breakthrough

I remember the day like it was yesterday—the day my hardened heart began to crack.

We were at a park with a playground. I pushed a little Latino boy on the swing. Although he was younger than my adopted brother Mike was when he joined my family, he could have been a little Mike. It reminded me that Mike, too, had once been a little boy on a swing.

The shoot ended and the social worker and little boy were walking to their car as I walked to mine. I looked over my shoulder. They were holding hands. A tiny hand grasping the big solid adult hand. The sun was shining down. Tears welled up. I saw just a little boy. Not the trauma, not the past, not his parents, not my brother. I saw an innocent boy.

Perhaps we are all he has.

I knew then I had a mission far bigger than just producing a weekly TV program. It wasn't just about doing the job, putting in the time, or being an unbiased journalist.

It was about changing lives, changing families, and just maybe, changing entire generations.

Recently, Editor Allison called my attention to the story of Queen Esther from the Old Testament. Esther started on a journey never expecting that God had some bigger purpose in mind for her. "For such a time as this" is an oft-used phrase that comes from this story.

That's how I felt when I looked at that little boy walking hand-in-hand with his social worker. Not like Esther, but like someone who suddenly realized I could use my work for greater good. Perhaps this kid and more like him had a fighting chance. Just maybe we could reach one little boy before it was too late. Just maybe we could find the right match. I wondered what would happen if we didn't fight for him. Just maybe there was a providential reason for why I was in this place at this time.

> "Three million cases of child abuse are reported each year."
>
> Project Nightlight

A New Lease on Life

With every child we profiled, the battle that waged in my heart about adoption was being conquered. But, it didn't happen overnight.

Mid-career these issues came crashing down. I was a whirling mess of emotions and didn't know why.

I worked in what many considered to be a glamorous and celebrated world. Yet, I'd created a lonely life. I often said "no" to friends when they invited me out and lived a life alone. I was a workaholic, career gal. Childless and unmarried, I had long ago moved away from family. My drink of choice was work and I drank it in heavy and hard. Few knew of this, certainly not the public.

I'd work through the tough times and wipe away the tears. I'd pray for answers to the questions that tortured my soul. In public, I seemed to have it all; I was Christine Devine, an award-winning news anchor. In private, I was a woman who waged a war of emotions and in dark days trudged through life wearing concrete boots.

As I sought answers to my questions there were many who held my hand ever so tightly. My mom would take a call at a moment's notice. She always had a spiritual word of wisdom that would send sunshine my way. My baby sister Danielle carried much of my weight. Seems she should have been the big sis. My financial team held down the fort on the business end. Dr. Pat Allen rocked my relationship world. I poured through self-help books and religious readings. So much so my co-anchor once chuckled, "Christine. You need to put down those books, stop analyzing yourself, and grab a good novel."

Little did I know I'd find so many answers in a man named Will Wong. Little did he know what he was in for when he took the job of Program Coordinator for the Freddie Mac Foundation's Wednesday's Child program.

> Life is a lease isn't it? I never thought of it that way but it's true. There's truly no guarantee and there will be many new segments in one's life where we, they, will all fail and succeed many times over. Adoption provides that chance to grow. Just because they're adopted doesn't mean that their life will be perfect or they will be perfect. It's not a magic filter that makes kids perfect. It's a guarantee perhaps of a place to belong and make those mistakes in the comfort of a family unconditionally and a place to celebrate life's successes when they do happen. Devine, there's no such thing as happily ever after, without life's challenges one cannot strive to overcome, without challenges or obstacles, how does one gauge they've succeeded? Will's Words of Wisdom.

The Captains of Team WC
Social Worker Will Wong and Christine

Chapter 4

Watchdog Will—Superstar Social Worker

He's the Starsky to my Hutch, the Cagney to my Lacey, the Mulder to my Scully, the Booth to my Brennan, the Robin to my Batman. These are of course famous TV partnerships. Perhaps you've watched the *X-Files*, *Bones*, or comic's dynamic duo? That's what Will Wong is to me. My partner in... Well, you get it!

Will is one example of the many people it takes to produce Wednesday's Child. There are numerous social workers, sponsors, "Dream Day" donors, photographers, editors, and of course the kids themselves. Will, however, is the main man and my unsung hero.

While I get to be the face of Wednesday's Child, Will is working tirelessly behind the scenes to make it all happen. A skilled listener and a warm, wonderful sage due to his years of social work, you might say that Will is the Obi-Wan Kenobi to my Luke Skywalker. He's just like that Jedi knight in *Star Wars* schooling an unskilled kid in many a battle, personally and professionally, including one involving my own birth father.

However, Will and I weren't always a dynamic duo. In fact, our intro was rather rough. Will had been assigned to take over the program, he was the latest in a string of coordinators and frankly I was disappointed over having yet another new person. He was at minimum the fourth person to run it. From then on, I'd beg the county for consistency. For me, it was a matter of insight, knowledge, safety and security. After all, we were dealing with a very sensitive matter and I appreciated a powerful person willing to stand up to me. Will recalls our first meeting.

Meeting Christine

> Admittedly I was not fully aware of what this program was until I was assigned. We have so many specialized functions at DCFS that it's very easy to get compartmentalized and focus on your area of expertise. The powers that be assured me that there was 'nothing to it' and not to worry. If my first day on the job was any indication, they were wrong.
>
> That first day was a Wednesday's Child shoot, and I introduced myself to Christine on location before the child and the child's social worker arrived. Christine asked me if I was the social worker, and I said yes. She was warm and friendly and I'll admit I was a bit awestruck at meeting her. As a county employee, I considered myself a commoner when it came to working with the pros on Fox 11 news, especially with Christine Devine. She was like princess royalty to me!

Herein lies the confusion. Will wasn't just any social worker. Unbeknownst to me, he was my new partner. I got no warning, no insight, no proper introduction. I was ticked. Will continues:

> In retrospect, I can see where we got off on the wrong foot with that miscommunication. She just banged out the shoot as I observed from the background trying to wrap my head around the method, the process and procedures. At the end of the shoot, I clarified with Christine that I was the new Wednesday's Child program coordinator. I felt the room go cold as her demeanor visibly changed. I had a lot of questions, but as I tried to engage in a conversation it was clear

> she didn't want to talk to me, and left as quickly as she could.
>
> I'm trained at reading between-the-lines and deciphering non-verbal signals, and I immediately sensed there was something wrong, and whatever it was, it was going to make my job extremely difficult.
>
> In my agency, once you transfer to a new assignment, it's at least a year before you can put in for another transfer. I went home, told my wife about my day and said '...this is going to be one very (#$&*!) long year!'

In my defense, I probably hadn't allotted for the time to break-in someone new at that moment, nor was I looking to once again go through it. In my apology, I should have made life a little easier for this man. He deserved my respect.

To say I (unfairly) put Will to the test might be an understatement. We roar about it today, but back then we went at it a bit. Will remembers all too well...

"I was accustomed to working in confrontational environments. Anyone who has a social worker in their lives usually doesn't have a choice, and I'm accustomed to working with involuntary clients, so when it came to Devine, I must have thought at some point... tough you-know-what lady, I'm here, deal with it."

> "When a prospective parent is considering a child that has been taped I can have the family go to the website and view the child/children. The taping of the children has made them seem much more than just their history. I know in the last year I have been able to make at least eight matches of children by using this method.
>
> Kim Felder
> Wendy's Wonderful Kids Recruiter

Will proved a worthy opponent in the ring. In fact, he won. Before long he saw behind my smoke and mirrors.

Little did he know, he would be tapped to counsel not only the kids, but me too.

Every Child Matters

Will went to work first and foremost for the children. I grew to respect his strength, experience and education, at the same time his tenacity and tenderness. We began to build WC into what it is today.

I came to see that as program coordinator Will didn't have a problem rolling up his sleeves and doing the "grunt" work as that was the core of who he was… a social worker. He's been a social worker for seventeen years, and by the time this book is published twelve of those years will have been spent with the County of Los Angeles.

He poured countless hours into Wednesday's Child on the job and off. For example, he created a photo program so that each and every kid gets great photos of our shoots. A budding photographer, Will shoots the stills himself, prints 'em up and gets 'em to the kids and our "Dream Day" sponsors. As kids in foster care move around that kind of stuff can get forever lost. Some never see themselves grow up through the memory of a photograph. As for the sponsors, I always smile when I see one has proudly displayed our photos on their company wall. The Freddie Mac Foundation loved this photo program so much I understand they're asking all their cities do it as well.

> "When we first saw the segment on Emilio and Alex on the Wednesday's Child website, we played it over and over again, studying their every word and move!"
>
> Ted Persky, Adoptive Parent

Over time, we saw our program changing how people view kids in the foster care system. Children come to life on the screen. The laughter, hopes and dreams in their own words, their innocence and world view. It all comes to life on Wednesday's Child. People get to see that these are real, living, breathing children just like any other child and they have hopes of belonging just like any person on this planet. We take time and energy to develop shoots personal to them, we call those our "Dream Days".

Every child needs to know that they matter. Children in foster care generally don't feel they are worthy and the projection from society at large tells them that they are not worthy. The biggest message is that they are worth it all and deserving.

Will says the value to the kids is that they will always know someone tried to help them find a family. That someone gave them an opportunity to advocate for themselves. That someone actually did believe in them. We gave them an opportunity to tell their story, to be validated.

And the Walls Came Tumblin' Down

The story of Wednesday's Child was being written while the story of my life was being changed. Soon, barriers were breaking down on all sides of me, and Will seemed intent on chipping away at the walls.

We'd worked together long enough to now be a team. A team meant a relationship. A relationship meant a friendship was forming. And a friendship meant you noticed birthdays and holidays. Will started with the gifts if I recall correctly.

One gift Will gave me was a teddy bear. It was brown, with curly soft hair. The judges in court offered each child a tiny soft bear on adoption day. The bear broke the ice and turned a cold courtroom into a place of love and kindness as adopting families took a bold new step. At the time I was cordial and thanked Will for the thoughtful gift. Inside, a hint of outrage welled up.

Why was this grown man giving me a teddy bear? Did he think I was a child?

At first, I was angry. I was a long-time news anchor, a bright educated woman, not a little girl. For a moment, I hated Will for not seeing a seasoned career gal. Then, I loved him for having the courage to hang in there, for seeing the heart of who I really was.

I'd come to reveal bits and pieces of my life to my WC colleague and he noticed everything. Over time, he put those pieces together. Will knew I had never met my birth father, and that my (adoptive) dad had drowned in a scuba diving accident. I was father-less and longed for that protective parent, that caring, kind man who'd watch over me. Don't get me wrong, Will primarily plays the role of obnoxious little brother, therapist, good friend, smart-aleck colleague, and the all-business social worker. Yet on this particular day he played a friend who understood, if not a father-figure role.

Although I came to cherish the teddy bear, I still felt uncomfortable that someone was seeing beneath the facade I tried so hard to maintain. Will was all about meeting the needs of our kids, those spoken and those left unsaid. He had an uncanny way of getting to the heart of an issue—and that day he got closer to the heart of mine.

> It's easy to say that 'still waters run deep' when you're dealing with someone who doesn't want to talk about what's really on their mind, someone who consistently constructs barriers to keep you at a distance. Yet, I didn't back down. I just kept on pressing with my opinions and contributions. I think at some level Christine respected me for that. I was just there, I kept at it and I think I proved to her that I was committed to what I was doing. I think that's when she started to let her guard down and let me in, too.

Props to Social Workers Everywhere

During all of this teddy-bear gift giving, I would meet two more men who would help change my life. Actually, one man and one young boy. Will was there through it all. WC works because of Will Wong. As I pass on the credit, Will is quick to share it with his colleagues, too.

> It's the field social workers who are the real heroes and inspiration that make this happen each and every day. Let them not be forgotten. They are the ones who refer kids to me for WC. The majority who do this work go unnoticed each and every day, often with much ill-informed public criticism. When I started with DCFS, the number of children receiving our services was over 50,000. It is now less than 30,000, thanks to the work being conducted by social workers each and every day. This is something that doesn't make the news. I MUST have props for my people. I am still one of them after all, not just Wednesday's Child Will.

On a professional note, Will is inching toward his tenth year with Wednesday's Child. He's one year shy of it. I'll go on record saying that I largely credit him with our success as he has also brought out the better in me. On a personal note, I say thank you, Obi-Wan.

"Your Wednesday's Child is extremely important. It gives others a chance to see the value of a human life."

Pamela, WC viewer

"A lot of us sleep better at night because there are people like you who care enough to do something good, and right."

Bo, WC viewer

"I have so much respect for you for doing Wednesday's Child and that has really motivated me to get out of self and be of service."

Gil, WC viewer

Jared at his "Dream Day" news shoot

Chapter 5

Meeting Jared

The Jared I see in my dreams is older than when we first met. Laughing, joking and smiling (despite his bulky silver braces). A thin teenage boy, he is lanky, his hair a tussled brown. He wanted to be a pro-baseball player.

When we met, Jared was a nine-year-old boy in foster care. It was about eight years into the Wednesday's Child project, and WC had yet to become a household favorite in Southern California.

At the time, Jared was still merely another assignment. I was still just doing my job.

None of these kids had yet to really own my heart.

A Gift Unlike Any Other

Christmas often means home for the holidays. For Jared, it meant a WC shoot date. Will coordinated everything. He thought the kid would be a perfect fit for a "Dream Day" with LA's pro-hockey team, the Los Angeles Kings. Will saw Jared as a spunky, athletic little guy willing to try most anything. The team of hockey players was hosting a kids Christmas party and Jared would be their VIP guest.

Jared was partnered with player Bryan Smolinsky. Bryan was a 6'1" 200 pound center who looked larger than life in his hockey uniform and elevated ice skates. We met the real guy,

Bryan in street clothes. It was a normal guy from Ohio who welcomed this little boy.

The day was a hit from the first moment. Bryan presented Jared with his very own pint-sized hockey jersey... of course, with Bryan's number on it.

"Oh WOW!" exclaimed Jared. The guys walked the Kings' locker room and then took to the ice. In the interview I'd asked Jared if he'd skated before. He said "yes" with his big wide grin, his front teeth jutting out. I later learned it was a lie... but a good one at that. You'd have never known he'd never been on ice. This crazy athletic kid just jumped right out there and went for it. He just skated his little heart out. That was Jared for ya!

The party was a mere backdrop for the personal profile. We wanted to know all about Jared. Prospective parents would be watching. It was Jared's chance to tell his story. I'd ask about school, hobbies, what he wanted to be when he grew up. The tough question for me always came when it was time to ask what a child wanted when it came to a forever family. I always choke up on that one. Some children say something as basic as "a family that's really fun and takes me places." Others want "a nice family." A few want a rich one. Some go really deep revealing a bit of their painful past. Sometimes, the social worker would speak on the child's behalf, especially if the child was too young or too shy.

Jared was neither!

As I look back, a favorite photo won't let me forget that day. The photo that begins this chapter reveals Jared sitting on the hockey bench off the ice wearing his purple-white-and-black oversized Kings jersey. His little head is cocked up. His hair spiky. At that moment he is an innocent little boy. Bright eyed. Excited. Happy. Friendly. Fun.

Jared was one cool kid.

Remember this was Christmas. So, of course, a Christmas party had to have Santa and plenty of presents. There was present upon present! Bryan piled 'em high in Jared's arms. The little boy with his thin little legs could barely walk, and certainly couldn't even see around the big stack.

It was a great day for a kid who'd seen more trauma than any kid should see ever in a lifetime. This was a "Dream Day" indeed, but not only for Jared.

A Christmas Dream Come True

Little did I know that it was also going to be a very special Christmas Day for a certain couple looking to adopt, Maureen and Dean Thomas. This year December 25 took on new meaning. They'd stay up late to watch the ten o'clock news that night. They'd be watching Jared's WC profile story.

While the Thomas' had already been doing the work to adopt, the news of this WC broadcast came as a sudden surprise. They got the call just one day before... on Christmas Eve. Their social worker had great news, they had been matched in the system with a young boy, and they needed to tune in to the news the next night.

As I anchored the Wednesday's Child segment, Maureen and Dean sat at attention as Jared's story appeared. It was love at first sight. "As soon as we saw him, we knew we had to fight to get him," said Maureen. "We looked at each other and said... that's him. That's our child."

Maureen noticed Jared was articulate with "definite thoughts on helping other people." She felt a kindred spirit as the nine-year-old boy talked of wanting to be a firefighter. "Both my husband and I had been involved with children for years, and this child looked as if he would be a perfect match for our family lifestyle of giving back."

That Christmas would be like none other for this couple from Downey, California and a little boy in foster care. Maureen would go on to call Jared, "her Christmas gift."

Jared Meets His Forever Family

After the segment aired I was "officially" out of the picture, my job was done. But that didn't mean the adoption wheel had stopped turning, it just meant I was out of the loop.

As adoption efforts went forward, it was time for the Thomas's to meet Jared in person. Maureen describes the visit as "awkward." There were social workers on both ends, theirs and Jared's, and his foster mother.

A moment, however, stood out as Maureen and Dean arrived at their meet location. She said it had been pouring rain that morning and the little boy came out to the car. "He told us to come in out of the rain." While they waited for the social workers to arrive, the couple got in some personal time with Jared. "We had perhaps fifteen minutes with him one on one, where he showed us his treasures, spoke a little about himself, and we got comfortable with each other."

That visit went well enough that it led to more visits and eventually Jared being placed in the Thomas home.

That's about the time I got the call.

Jared Makes the Call

I was in my office prepping for the night's newscast. As the 10 p.m. anchor for Los Angeles news station, KTTV Fox 11, my early evening duties were to study wire copy, monitor breaking news, write news stories, and work on Wednesday's Child. My phone lit up with a message on the machine.

As I played back the recording a tiny voice piped up.

"Hi, it's Jared." The little boy left a phone number for me to call.

I studied the number. No kid had ever called me. I remembered Jared from a shoot we did around Christmas. It was now months later. *Why was he calling? And how did this young boy have my number?*

Turns out, this clever little guy had asked for my business card on the day of our shoot many months before. I was caught off-guard as no kid had asked for my number before. The county maintains privacy and abides by strict court orders until the children are adopted. The county remains the go-between for me and the children, and I always defer to my WC coordinator. Caught by surprise and not wanting to be rude, I had reached into my purse and honored young Jared's request, and gave him my card. I guess I figured he was only nine years old, what harm could come of it? *Sure, the kid can have my card.* I figured it would end up in the trash anyway.

Apparently, I was wrong.

I returned his call and discovered that Jared had exciting news. He wanted me to know he'd found a forever family.

"I'm getting adopted!" he squealed.

A Follow-up

Like any good reporter I seized the moment, asking new-mom-to-be, Maureen, a string of questions.

"Could we come to adoption day? Could we shoot another story on Jared? Could we do a follow-up after our initial recruitment segment? Could we offer proof Wednesday's Child was working?"

Maureen was very receptive to the idea, and I was over-the-moon! We would show viewers that yes, indeed, our children were getting out of the system and into safe, permanent homes. They were finding families!

As for family follow-ups, we'd only covered two others in all of our years of showcasing children in foster care. This time was different. My heart had been touched, my mind inquisitive. With one eye open I tip-toed through a new door. I was curious. *Who was this kid who had the courage to call? Who were these people wanting to adopt? Would it work? Would it last?*

I had reason to question and it was purely personal. Part of me wanted—needed—to know more about this kid and his new family.

It was a perfect follow-up story.

Adoption Day

Our camera was staked outside the courthouse awaiting this soon-to-be family. They emerged from the parking garage looking ever so stylish. Mom, Maureen, in a green dress perfect for her Irish skin and red hair. Dad, Dean, walked proudly in his uniform adorned with medals. And then there was Jared. How dashing he looked in a black tux, he was now ten years old, yet he looked ten feet tall. Jared tilted his head in shy embarrassment, but his face fought off a smile. Our camera rolled.

It was wonderful to witness this start to finish. A judge officiated the adoption. Jared's new last name would be Thomas. He would be the only son of a couple who chose not to have children for medical reasons. Mom presented Jared with a ring to symbolize the relationship. Jared later chuckled, "I thought I was getting married." As Mom said in the ceremony, "With this ring you are now part of our family."

Later that day, new Mom Maureen tearfully reminded me they first saw Jared on TV on Christmas Day.

"He was our Christmas gift."

Happy Birthday

We'd captured much of Jared's story on tape, beginning with his Wednesday's Child news profile, then his adoption, and shortly thereafter we attended his first official birthday as a "Thomas."

Jared was turning eleven, and his birthday party was held at an ice skating rink. So inspired by his Wednesday's Child shoot with LA's pro-hockey team, Jared had taken up the sport. In fact, his computer login was hockeyjared. "I wanna play for the Kings!" he exclaimed. "Only the L.A. Kings!" The new mom and dad hosted the birthday bash, their first as adoptive parents.

What a joy it was to see Jared surrounded by friends. He skated as if he'd been doing it his whole life. Mom and dad beamed with pride. I was thrilled to see him, them, so happy.

Yes, he was a special kid, but little did I know he would take up residence in my heart as well, *for the next several years.*

A Year of Honors

Jared wasn't just any child. He'd started to inch his way into my heart and soul. Initially, he was like most any other child I'd profiled. I did my job. Covered his Wednesday's Child day with the same zest as most every shoot. Jared's excitement, however, was infectious. His grin went from ear-to-ear. And quite simply, he never went away. Eventually, he too saw through my shell with a little-kid curiosity way beyond his years. It was, however, a relationship that built over time, so for now, we go back to the beginning.

Jared and his family were becoming regulars at our annual Six Flags Magic Mountain reunion. He followed me around like a shadow. Maureen had said that I looked like the Pied Piper. "A good one, I hope!" I had laughed.

At the reunion one year, Maureen gathered a small crowd as Jared presented me with a plaque that read, "AMAZING PERSON" award. Outwardly, I was thrilled with the gesture of the little boy and thanked him appropriately. Inwardly, I was mortified.

No! I am not an amazing person. I'm just doing my job. I'm covering my assignment.

They had no idea of the demons I wrestled with when it came to adoption.

While I may have been good on camera, the real amazing people were the kids of Wednesday's Child. On our shoots, I believed every child deserved a chance and I supported the people wanting to adopt. But I knew I was *not* amazing.

Maureen asked me later why I never aired that moment. Truth was, the emotion of it was too real. The little guy had captured my heart, and that wasn't supposed to happen. This was a job, it was not personal. I wasn't going to go there.

I hung it on my wall, but I kept the plaque private. I wanted to earn the title.

As time went on, the Thomas family surfaced yet again. They'd been chosen by The Freddie Mac Foundation, our sponsor, as their Family of the Year. The Thomas' would be photographed and appear in the Foundation's annual update. It was worth a mention on the news too. I was stunned to see the photo Maureen had e-mailed to me. Jared was growing up. It was a picture of him in a small airplane with his dad. Dean was a pilot in the Civil Air Patrol. Father and son looked happy.

About that same time, I was being honored by the Los Angeles Police Department as I'd been selected "Humanitarian of the Year." Feeling slightly shy about the whole thing, I asked the Thomas family to join me, plus with Dean being Civil Air Patrol, I thought they might like the LAPD atmosphere and this event at the academy. I asked our "Family of the Year" to represent.

Dean showed up in uniform, Jared in a suit and tie. How smart he looked. How big he was getting. How shy he still was around me! A striking father and son, and proud momma too.

I quietly made notice of the changes in Jared. He stood taller and now wore his hair spiky and longer. He was no longer that wide-eyed little boy. I was pleased to see his growth, pleased to see him suit up and attend an event on behalf of WC.

"Even though Jared had an adopted family, that didn't stop us from adopting him as part of our gang. Whether he was accompanying Christine to a black-tie dinner or rolling up his sleeves to help us with one of our many projects, we could always count on Jared for being helpful, respectful and thoughtful."

Anchor/Reporter
Wendy Burch, Founder,
The Good News Foundation

VIP Guests

Receiving the Humanitarian of the Year honor was so appreciated. That public recognition, which included Jared and his family, opened the door for a new chapter in my life. I realized I no longer had to attend these events alone. The adopted children of Wednesday's Child might like a night out on the town, or to sit VIP at a fancy luncheon. I was grateful to have these guests as I'd attended many an event alone. I loved attending community events and charity fundraisers but they can be long and tedious. I attend so many I feared exhausting friends and family.

I was thrilled when the Thomas' would come. That grew into a pattern, as the Thomas' were always good to go. In fact, they became my always-dependable family, going to several events with me every year.

From then on, I slowly started to use future events to share the wealth.

Jared was always my go-to guy. I'd throw out an invite and he always RSVP'd, "Yes."

It was an opportunity for him to feel important, to be recognized, to make a difference. I introduced him to the audience at every speech, walked him up to the Mayor, the Police Chief, pro athletes, and famous actors. I wanted him to meet people in power. I'd ask them to offer a quick word of wisdom. I wanted Jared to see a future bigger than he ever imagined. He accepted every invitation so it was easy. Jared would be the first to arrive and the last to leave. He soaked up every moment, welcomed every introduction, and listened to every adult.

The kid was like a sponge.

Jared and his family take a cruise

A growing boy, Jared at News Emmys

Chapter 6

A Wednesday's Child Grows Up

The Thomas' were proof; adopting older kids in county foster care was working! They'd led the way to erasing the stigma, and their new son had become a domestic adoption shining star. No, he wasn't perfect... he was a teenager. But he offered hope to every family wanting to adopt, considering domestic adoption, or who had adopted. He offered hope to every child in foster care waiting to be adopted. Hope that they, too, might find a loving, safe, permanent place to call home. That's what domestic adoption is all about, rescuing children from a painful past. Abuse, abandonment or neglect... the reasons a child is placed into foster care by the courts.

Jared had become more than the job. I let him into my personal life. He and mom came to my home for a huge Christmas party, even brought cookies they had baked together. I had become engaged to Sean McNabb, a musician and actor (and my Rockstar!) and we went to Jared's sixteenth birthday party. He came to my fiancé's birthday pool party, and sometimes when Sean was unavailable, Jared would accompany me to events. I was surprised that as a teenager, he found these events fun given all the long speeches. Whether it was the Mayor's Prayer Breakfast, the news Golden Mic awards, or even philanthropic charity dinners, Jared was always game to go.

Legacy

His parents believed in giving back to the community, a belief I had long shared as well, and I wanted to foster in Jared the value of volunteering. One Saturday he stuffed gift bags for the news ladies "Good News Foundation" silent auction. One year he offered to help the younger kids at our WC Magic Mountain reunion. That particular year, he was turning sixteen and instead of running around the park, he stuck by my side and helped the children. If a child was riding alone, he would jump on the ride with him. If there were a bunch of little kids, he would be the big kid on the ride assuring them all was okay. Jared became our first unofficial Wednesday's Child ambassador. That was amazing! He got it! *To whom much is given, much is expected!*

On that same morning we honored Jared's sixteenth birthday. The staff was waiting as families started to arrive. Social workers gathered around and we all sang Happy Birthday. He smiled, not able to hide his braces. He blew out the candles on not cake, but cupcakes. I grabbed my mic for a quick interview.

"Why are you volunteering today?" I inquired.

"Because of all you've done for me. I want to give back," he said assuredly.

I was so proud of him. I was grooming him for great things, and he was becoming a good little humanitarian. I'd made sure to introduce him to Pastor Rick Warren at one event, the author of the bestselling book, *A Purpose Driven Life*.

Growing Up

As he got older, Jared would outgrow the suits Maureen would buy him. One year he'd have braces, the next year not. He went through puberty, his voice changed, he suffered through the acne stage, grew tall and lanky. And often wherever I spoke at public events, my trusted sidekick would go, too. He'd often hang out at awards events with the local news anchors. I think he was most thrilled to meet Dodger Tommy Lasorda at the News Emmys. Jared had since left hockey for baseball and dreamed of a career as a pitcher. A moment stood out in my mind. We walked through the crowd that night and someone yelled out, "Hi Jared!" By the end of each event we attended, everyone knew Jared.

Over time, we'd gone from professional to personal, and one day I woke up and realized that something miraculous had happened.

I realized domestic adoption *could* work, and it *was* working, all around me.

Perhaps I projected the personal. Or perhaps I was wise enough now to be the big sister to Jared that I'd wished I could have been to Mike.

Amidst all that self-revelation, combined with all of Will's teddy-bear-giving advice and concern, I realized somewhere in the middle of living that I had actually started living. That it is possible to have hope, find healing, and experience love no matter where you've been, or what you've done.

At sixteen, Jared was the brother I wished I'd had, the son I was yet to have, and the supportive friend everyone deserved to have, all rolled into one.

Jared, Maureen, and Dean attend LAPD awards

We share a laugh on Jared's 16th birthday

Chapter 7

Losing Jared

Little Rock, Arkansas held a special place in Maureen's heart. It was home. Where she went to college. It meant a best friend she called family. She was now retired and wanted to offer Jared a better life, away from the big city.

Maureen's pension would allow the family to build a dream home in Little Rock, from the ground up. It would be their new future. Jared would finish his last years of high school in the tiny town of Beebe, Arkansas. In the meantime, Dean would temporarily stay in L.A.

The finality of it all came as a bit of a shock. Maureen broke the news to me while at dinner. She'd asked if she and Jared could meet up with me for a quick bite. I was silenced by the news of their move, but trusted that Mom had to do what was best.

This was the first time she'd come to me like this and I knew it was a meaningful moment. I promised Jared we'd have him back for a visit. It felt hollow but certainly wasn't impossible. I couldn't believe this meal at a Mexican restaurant might be our last for a long time. I was sad to lose my side-kick.

"Our Wednesday's Child reunion is just a few months away, you'll be back for that, right Maureen?" She had no doubts. "Of course we'll be back. We wouldn't miss it for the world."

We said our good-byes at the valet. I returned to work for the newscast feeling a little at a loss.

The Wednesday's Child annual reunion came and went. Maureen and Jared never made it out. Blame the stress of the move and obligations of starting a new life. Jared was making new friends but also was having some trouble. At first he was refusing to go to school. I listened by phone to Maureen's struggle, and then spoke with Jared.

I'm surprised I don't recall the conversation more. I was probably lightly lecturing Jared about the importance of school and a high school diploma. He politely stayed on the phone, perhaps out of respect and obligation. I remember that he was so quiet; I feared I was losing him.

"Jared, I've got to hit the road now, but I'm going to call you soon, okay?"

"Yeah, sure, see you then."

Just before hanging up, Jared suddenly piped up and demanded, "Hey, when are you guys getting married?"

Jared had always liked Sean, and his concern for our future made me smile, gave me hope that the Jared I knew and loved was still there.

It was the last time I would ever speak to my sweet friend.

The Call

A few days later, my phone rang at 4 a.m. It was Maureen. Jared had been in an auto accident. He and a friend had gone out for a Sunday night drive, Jared was the passenger. An older teen had a truck and took them both to see the property for the new Thomas house. It was a mild, rainy night on a dark country road. The truck slid off the slick road and slammed into a tree. While the driver had cuts and scratches he was okay. Jared, however, was badly hurt. He'd lost oxygen. There was brain damage.

Not wanting to believe, I flew out to Arkansas. I was convinced I'd be the savior. I was convinced I'd walk into that hospital room and we'd connect once again. Jared would open his eyes and pop right out of that hospital bed. He'd play baseball, go to college, get married, have babies. And I'd get to be there through it all.

Upon arriving at Little Rock Children's Hospital I received my reality check. Jared's pale, frail, lifeless body told the story. Maureen's tears echoed the truth. Doctor visits to the room left little hope, as Jared struggled on life support.

A Final Birthday with Jared

Wednesday, May 27 was Jared's seventeenth birthday. I'd spent his sixteenth birthday with him and his family, and it was devastating to see him this way on this day. A lovely woman from Arkansas Children's Hospital waltzed in with birthday balloons. (Food wasn't allowed, so no cake.) A few nurses gathered 'round... and we sang "Happy Birthday." Seemed odd to sing "happy" birthday as there seemed little to be happy about, except for the fact that we could be with Jared one more day.

As Maureen stood vigil in Jared's room in the ICU, I was forced to return to L.A. Knowing Dean was on his way and would be there soon, I said good-bye to her and to Jared, who remained unconscious.

Two weeks later, our beloved Wednesday's Child ambassador passed from this life to the next, leaving an incomprehensible void in so many lives, yet at the same time inspiring us to make a difference in our own lifetime, because he had certainly made a difference in his.

Young Jared, forever in our hearts

Chapter 8

Remembering Jared

Although Maureen and Dean's pain must have been ten-fold, Jared's death washed over me like an icy, ocean wave. I was stunned, saddened, and devastated. Grief numbed me. My buddy, the little guy I was mentoring for big things, was no more.

The child I had grown to love was gone.

Jared exited my life just as he'd entered it—with his story once again on TV.

We'd had many firsts on Wednesday's Child, our first adoption, our first kid in high school, first in college, and our first follow-up profile. But never a death. This too was a first. We'd never had to say a permanent goodbye on Wednesday's Child.

Maureen pointed out that Jared was born on a Wednesday, profiled on the news on a Wednesday, and died on a Wednesday.

Over three hundred people attended his memorial in Downey, California. Think about that. We were not in school session, and Jared had moved across the country to Arkansas several months before. So, it wasn't as if the high school emptied out and all went to the service. It was a mix of the many lives he had touched. His social worker, his baseball coach, kids from church, colleagues from Fox 11 News, and of course, Will Wong. Most I did not know. Funny... a few approached me saying they hadn't really believed Jared when he said he was hangin' out with "the news lady."

The Next Chapter

As the shock of a sudden death slowly bubbled down, I began to ponder some questions. With a vision to keep Jared's memory alive I began to wonder...

Could Jared leave behind a legacy? Could his passing be used for good? Could he be a Wednesday's Child ambassador in death as he had been in life?

The loss of Jared brought the memories of Mike to the forefront. I asked myself,

Could we do more for children walking their walk?

The answer was yes. A resounding yes!

And so began the next chapter in my unplanned work with adoption. When Jared passed away, I turned to writing to console my heart and refresh my spirit. Call it a way of coping. I poured my heart and soul out onto the pages. I realized we all have a story to tell. With Jared guiding me from the heavens above we would tell the stories of domestic adoption, share our wealth of knowledge. We would bring our families together. We would share ideas, give some parenting tips and tools, be a guide for anyone wanting to adopt.

After fifteen years of adoption work, it was time to take our story beyond Los Angeles, California. I began to realize my own legacy, something our Wednesday's Child advocates were learning as well, the time-honored truth that it really is better to give than to receive—that giving back truly does feel amazing—that true philanthropy isn't just about giving money—but time and love as well.

An "Ah-ha" Moment

Something happened to me after Jared's memorial service as I began to think about my dear friend and his family. I returned to work that day with a passion and fire inside. One that burned like nothing else had in the past fifteen years. It was an energy that had long been extinguished due to life's disillusionments and routine.

Never again would I take life for granted, wallow in my sorrows, or live without energy. I do believe we are all entitled to whine a little, complain about job, family, friends, and circumstances, for I believe that allows one to process and evoke change, but a time must come to move on. I swore to never again be satisfied with a simmering fire of existence. I vowed to be explosive—to live life to its fullest.

I remembered what I'd once said about what I'd want written on my epitaph, "She Made a Difference. It was time to make a difference.

The Birth of Our Book

I asked some of our families to share their journey, to teach us what works, and in some cases, what doesn't. I called on my team, TEAM WC!

I begin with my own family, our story of adoption and foster care, my mother, the man she married, and yes, my own adoption.

I would make public the story behind the story.

If Jared could bare his soul, so could I.

If Jared, in all his sweet innocence and beyond-his-years wisdom, could be strong enough to be vulnerable, so could I.

It all began with Christine Yara Lucas, a little girl who once was lost, but somehow along the journey found her way.

Sean, Christine and Pips

I think Jared had an old soul. There was something in his eyes that shined and showed what a special young man he really was.

I was looking forward to being there for him when he had questions that he might not have been comfortable asking his parents. I felt like I might be able to help him avoid some of the mistakes I made growing up.

Sometimes I felt like he was gonna ask me something but I wanted it to be on his terms. I knew at some point I wanted to have "the talk" with him, the one about the dangers of drugs and alcohol. I know from experience that you can waste a lot of time there. I once had a vision of taking him with me to an AA meeting as a visitor or observer, as I knew substance abuse had been an issue in his biological family.

One of the many great moments I remember was him playing air hockey with actress Dakota Fanning at an event we all attended. That kid could hang with anybody and it never seemed to faze him if they were famous or not. He just saw them as people like they are and I always admired that in him.

Maureen and Dean are such great parents and helped to make him the kind and unselfish young man he was. I have so much respect for them.

In many ways I think all of us were lucky to have had him in our lives as long as we did. He taught us a lot about humility and general human kind. I miss the little man. He was growing fast and would probably be taller than me by now.

You know, Billy Joel got it right in his song, "Only the Good Die Young." Jared will forever be in my heart and the 'Pipsers heart (our dog) as well. I will see him in the next life I hope.

God Bless,
Sean McNabb
(Christine's Fiancé)

1. News Emmy Night: Anchor Carlos Amezcua, Senior Exec. Producer Cheryl Carson, and Christine 2. Skylar Emma 3. Christine w/Brazilian Carnaval King 4. Christine and foster sister Terrisa (BT) Nguyen 5. Mom, Christine and sister Danielle 6. Christine and Sean on Oscar night

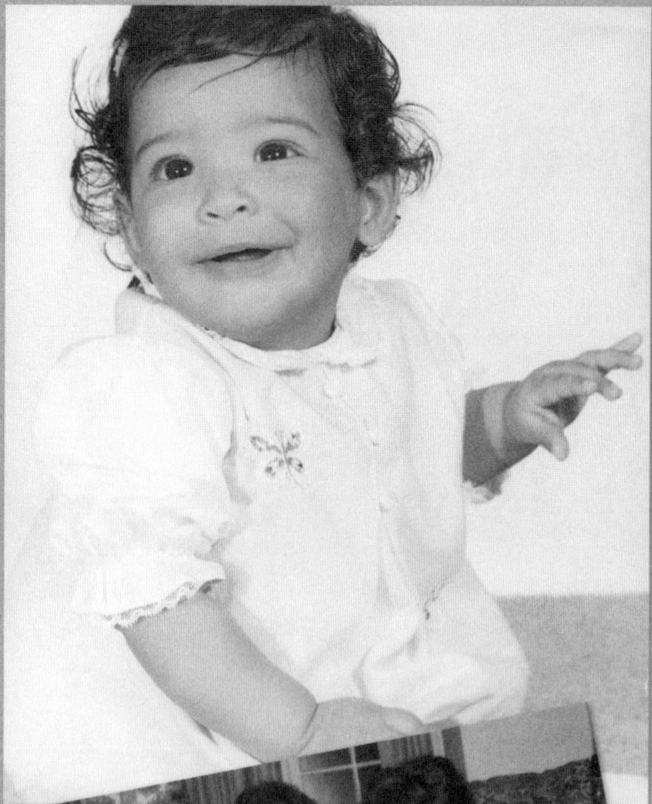

1. Christine's baby pic 2. Grandpa Julius Seufert, Mom, Grandma Dolores Seufert and baby Christine

1. Emmy night: Christine, Will & Naehi Wong, Wednesday's Child's Daysi 2. Christine with the Diaz kids at Dodger Night 3. Christine and Daysi present at Emmys 4. Magic Mountain reunion: Jared & Sierra 5. Kings Night: The Clivers: Deon, Carl, & Da'Vonn

1. Brooklyn shows off photo album on adoption day 2. Christine interviews Madison, Austin, & Joey 3. The Williams family on adoption day w/Judge Nash 4. The Silcock family 5. Reunion sign-in

PART TWO

Me and Mom at News Emmy night
(we won four!)

Chapter 9

My Forever Family—The Devine Family

"When President Kennedy announced the formation of the Peace Corps it was the answer to my dreams. I wanted to be of service in a third-world country..."

Much to my joy and surprise, my mom has started to document her days as a Peace Corps volunteer in Brazil. The years were 1963-1965, and history was in the making in this large South American country (including a non-violent coup!)

The girls in the Peace Corps lived in a tiny place on a hillside in the impoverished favelas. A black and white photo of "the girls," Mom, Carol, and Mary, takes me there and I fantasize about their experience.

My mother made for a fabulous photograph. Straight dark hair framed her round face, milky white skin, high cheekbones and a striking wide smile. She was thin and about 5' 4". Mom's beauty did not go unnoticed, except by her. The Peace Corps used her in their magazines, even on the cover. A photo collage on my wall is proof, and includes that Peace Corps magazine cover. Mom is kneeling, arm around a Brazilian toddler holding a doll. The child's hair is curly and unkempt, Mom wears a crisp white shirt and a big captivating smile. She was striking. Everyone notices Mom's beauty (and asks if that tattered looking little girl is me, and of course she is not). Mom looks gorgeous in those Peace Corps photos. Think Sophia Loren. I'm not the first to jump to that conclusion (and not the last.) Even the Brazilians would scream in delight "you look like that movie star!" In another brochure she happily plays a small guitar with two boys. In a following brochure a reader's comment was posted. "I never thought I'd have a Volunteer as a pin-up." I'm guessing this all came as a flattering surprise to my mom as she was sickly as a child and glam to this day is not her thing. Still, she found celebrity in Brazil, in more ways than one.

Mom's cover shot for Peace Corps magazine

That's where my mom met my birth father. As the story goes, he was an actor/dancer on a TV show in Brazil. He came from a mixed race family but was the darkest of all his siblings. Mom's colleague Mary married a Brazilian and he tells me my father was "very handsome." I'm guessing my father got great status in dating a pretty American girl.

To sum up what is surely a long, detailed, and dramatic story, Mom got engaged and pregnant. My grandmother was mortified and flew from Buffalo to Brazil. She was quite the eyesore, arriving in a bright yellow suit and matching floppy hat, shoes, AND handbag. She went there to talk everyone into going back to Buffalo. Mom's Peace Corps term was coming to an end any way. I'm told my birth father came to New York, but things ultimately didn't work out and he returned to Brazil about a month before I was born. For family reasons, I have no photo, have never seen him, and there is little discussion about him. Mom just simply moved on with the thought "I'm going to be the best parent I can be." I was born with his last name, Lucas. Christine Yara Lucas. Yara is Brazilian for "Goddess of Water" and it is all I have of my heritage there... and perhaps his dance gene. Zumba, anyone?

Mom and I lived with my German grandparents, Dolores and Julius Seufert, in upstate New York farm country. A town today, North Boston, that still only has a population of 4,000. Mom got a job with Teacher Corps, which placed teachers in Buffalo's inner-city. Grandma loved me with every ounce of her being and grandpa played protective father. All was well in my world.

I have a photo from that time that I love. It's in color, and I'm a baby surrounded by Mom, Grandpa and Grandma. This was my family. I loved my grandma and grandpa beyond belief. They were, perhaps, my favorite people on the planet and I just might have been theirs.

Grandpa was a man of honor in this tiny town. There was even a street named after his father, Seufert Street. Grandpa was a good guy in every way. Leader of the boy scouts, coached a baseball team, was a volunteer firefighter, a small-time farmer, and owned the area's first television store. He was known to offer his TV repair services and fresh vegetables free to those who couldn't pay.

Faith was important to my grandpa, and growing up, I can remember him reading Bible passages each morning. "I've read the Bible seven times," he'd said. A cherished family heirloom I have is an oversized leather bound Bible, the size you'd find in a museum preserved in a glass case, the pages embossed in gold, the photos in rich color. He was protestant, she Catholic, and that caused many a family rift forcing them to elope.

Mom's spirit for adventure and restless ways wouldn't keep her in this too-tiny town. She moved the two of us to Tucson, Arizona when I was two years old. That's where she met Jack Duane Devine, also a former Peace Corps volunteer. I was three when he became my dad.

He was getting a Political Science degree at the University of Arizona when he met Mom at a Peace Corps event. Never the traditionalists, they married a month later. My little sister Danielle (Dani) was born two years later. Dad was of Irish descent, from Nevada, and much to his mother's disappointment had abandoned his strict Mormon upbringing. Grandma Devine made sure there were constant invitations to return. Instead of a Mormon mission he'd served in the Army and then went into the Peace Corps. He taught school in a rural village in Tanzania, Africa. It was so remote that when Bobby Kennedy asked to visit the most remote village,

Dad's was it. Dad would go on to teach in the states, making education his life-long profession. He worked at Job Corps in the inner city, and as a high school principal. As a vice principal he was a national VP of the Year. Dad was a devoted educator.

Unanswered Questions

A product of Mom and Dad, Dani was white skinned like them, round faced and had Dad's thin blonde hair. I resembled my Brazilian birth father as I took on height, a narrow face, curly hair, brown skin, and long gangly arms. That issue alone caused many days in therapy and nagging questions. I've not met a child yet who isn't curious about their birth parent. I wondered why I looked so different from anyone else in the family. My mixed race (Anglo, Latin, black and native Brazilian) and foreign influence left me with no racial identity or ethnic place to call home. Despite my good upbringing and secure family, I will always have questions about my birth father, even a fairytale fantasy. That's a common thing with children who don't know a birth parent. We want to believe dad is a King and mom a Queen. I mentally asked questions, like...

Is he alive? What did he look like? What was his life like? Did he get married? Does he have children? Was he really famous? What might my life have been like had he remained in the picture? Would I live in Brazil? Would I visit? Would I have grandparents there too? Would he have been a great father? Would he have been proud of me now? Would I really want the answers? And what if he wasn't that knight in shining armor?

A United Nations Portrait

With their shared Peace Corps history, my parents had a passion for those in need, an interest in world affairs, and education was a priority. We would become a United Nations portrait.

Our family was productive and progressive. Dad was a responsible guy. He was dedicated to his jobs in the world of education. He was smart, educated, intelligent, and worldly. Dad had his master's degree and then a Ph.D. He wore the titles proudly, if not a tad arrogantly. He was even my high school principal. He valued smart. Dad was a voter registrar so there were always strangers at the house coming to register to vote. Mom was a teacher, my Girl Scout leader and a strong disciplinarian. To say my parents were present is an understatement.

We were a happy bunch. We had a great house. Middle class, cookie cutter, new. I always loved living in Arizona with its new construction. Not like back east with its old homes and rich history. A new home in Arizona meant no leaky roofs, no rust on the pipes, no dust hardened into cracks and corners. Everything was brand new. Mom could decorate to her heart's content, and she loved color. A royal blue carpet and couches the color of crimson red. Dad had zebra print curtains. His African masks on the wall told a story of their own. We had a big, blue, inviting swimming pool and a tall, sturdy swing set. A perfect, kid friendly home; all the neighborhood kids hung out at our house. Perhaps it was because Mom was an elementary school teacher that she knew kids and cool activities.

Life seemed perfect. I could walk to school. Wait for the ice cream truck. I had a crush on the neighborhood boy Steve. He was a red-head. My first kid-crush (one that alas was not returned by the way). I had friends who lived behind the Terraults, the Edens. They had lots of sisters of all ages. One summer they took me to Bible school. I played on the softball team their dad coached. My mom would cart us around town, to gymnastics, hula dance, ballet, and tennis. It was something different every summer. Mom wanted to expose us to many things, which kind of meant we were a "jack-of-all-trades" and master of none. She'd load all the neighborhood kids into our Volkswagen van. That was the time before car seats and seat belts. We'd sing and laugh all the way to wherever it was we were going, be it Girl Scouts, soccer, or an art program. The streets of Westside Phoenix were safe, the sun was bright, the weather warm. In the summer, Arizona was sizzling, and swim team made for wet, welcome relief from the heat. My little sister Danielle was a champion kid swimmer, yet efforts to encourage her to start pre-Olympic training (with 4 a.m. call times) were to no avail. Interestingly, she married an ASU swimmer, Lance Bedolla, and their daughter Skylar at two years old was already swimming like a fish.

I had such warm childhood memories. At least for the first decade of my life.

Life Changed

Then, my parents decided it would be good to have a boy in the family. They wanted to adopt someone in between the ages of my sister and me. I was ten and Dani was five. That's when eight-year-old Mike entered the picture. He was Mexican-American, further changing the family ethnic portrait.

Our first meetings were great. I'd be getting a little brother! I remember meeting at a McDonalds one time and going to an animal park another time. I remember returning home and telling the neighbor boy that Mike was, "the cutest little thing I'd ever seen." He was thin, brown skinned like me, had thick wiry hair, a big toothy smile and those to-die-for dimples.

At the animal park, I offered to buy Mike a stamp book. He asked for two. Even as a little boy, Mike was a gifted artist who could sketch your portrait or an animal in a tree. My mom recalls the time as though it were yesterday.

> As an only child, I had longed for brothers and sisters. So I knew that I wanted a really big family when I got married, and the children didn't necessarily need to be birth children. When Jack and I got married, I was delighted to learn that he wanted to adopt also. We had both been in the Peace Corps and felt that adopting children from third-world countries would be a good way to go. However, when we approached agencies dealing with foreign adoptions we were turned away, as at that time all the agencies were run by religious groups and we didn't fit their qualifications.

> With those rejections we decided to pursue an adoption of an older child in our area.
>
> Unfortunately, our social worker was new and was more impressed with our education and expectations for our children's education than she was with making sure the adoption was a good fit. She did not investigate what the child wanted, what might be best for him. So, we were paired with an eight-year-old Hispanic child who had a very high IQ.

Mike was placed with our family because the social worker said he was smart and we were bookworms. We learned later that books and education held little interest for him.

"What he needed was a sports family," Mom once said. "He needed to rough-house with other boys, and what he got instead were two sisters, two girls." My mom was convinced early on we were not a good fit, but my dad didn't want Mike to go through another disruption, so he decided to proceed with the adoption.

With that adoption, we were now family. The Devine family. Mom, Dad, Danielle, Mike, me and our poodle Serendipity (Dippy).

Two years after Mike's adoption dad took a new job. It was on a reservation in Arizona. It was a unique experience, and I have fond memories of hiking the scenic canyons and enjoying the snowy winters. But my mom says that's also where Mike was introduced to drugs by some older neighborhood boys.

Mike was only eleven and in the fifth grade. He was forever a changed person, and our life as a family would never be the same.

It became a world where drugs, crime, pain, fear and anger frequently bubbled to the surface, erupting and burning everything in its path. Then, retreating and cooling, only to return again.

I so love my editor on this book for she understands this dance of drama and chaos. We were a perfect fit and she helped me to understand that such a story does not just come with children from foster care, but can also be found in many a birth family, even her own. Allison Bottke wrote about her own journey with her drug addicted son in *Setting Boundaries with Your Adult Children, Six Steps to Hope and Healing for Struggling Parents*.

> We should never give up hope that our adult children will find a way out of the dark abyss of addiction. We should never stop encouraging them, emotionally supporting them, and loving them. And we should never stop praying for them. Miracles happen every day, and God will make a way where there seems to be no way. However, there is a difference between remaining hopeful and emotionally supportive and bearing acute financial responsibility of drug or alcohol rehab time and time again. There is a difference between helping and enabling, and we must learn to set healthy boundaries with our children, no matter what their age.[1]

Drug Abuse Enters Our World

From there, my memory of Mike is condensed into one ugly little ball. High school for me meant years of friends and school activities. Dad was the school principal and I was Daddy's little girl. I rode to work with him so I'd be the first kid there. I'd study, chat with teachers, practice dance routines. I loved being a part of it all. Over the years, I was on the track team, tennis team, Honors Society, a cheerleader, A-student, Student Government, and had the best boyfriend. He was on the football team at a neighboring school, student body President, had a job and a car! I was class Valedictorian and offered college scholarships.

During these years, Mike was largely stoned.

For Mike, school was torture.

His high school days were lackluster. I don't recall him getting good grades. Dad forced Mike to join ROTC, he thought the military training might shape him up. It didn't, it only added

1 Allison Bottke, *Setting Boundaries with Your Adult Children, Six Steps to Hope and Healing for Struggling Parents* (Eugene, OR: Harvest House Publishers, 2008), 189.

to his misery. Once a week he'd have to dress in military attire. I remember him trudging around campus in a dull and depressed demeanor.

We were polar opposites.

I was embarrassed for my father and the colleagues he had to face at school. I know Mike's troubles exhausted Mom to no end. No effort at discipline seemed to cure Mike from running to drugs. Danielle recalled, "Don't you remember the time I found a roach clip on my Teddy Bear ear? I gave it to you and you hid it?" While it frightened me at the time I now applaud Mom's no tolerance stance and effort at tough love. There was talk of sending him to a boarding school. At the time it all scared me so I buried myself in my books and felt great pressure to right Mike's wrongs. I excelled in school not just for the joy of it but perhaps to prove to others my parents were good parents... to make up for Mike.

Gone was the little boy I once described as "the cutest little thing I'd ever seen." Gone was my perfect little family. Buried was the natural born artist. Poor choices and drugs robbed me of a brother and my parents of a son.

My brother was no brother. He was a stoned out, withdrawn, empty shell.

And Mom and Dad were powerless. The pain of it all echoed through the chambers of my heart. It was a gaping wound in my soul. It left me tortured and twisting in the wind.

I can still see the cop car arriving at our house that first time. Once again, my mom recalls this time with heart-breaking clarity.

> Mike's intelligence made school easy for him until he started doing drugs. Then, instead of being highly motivated he became surely, oppositional, disrespectful and often obnoxious to be around.
>
> He started using marijuana at age eleven, and in retrospect I can now see where he was self-medicating for his painful self-image and equally painful childhood memories.

> Had any of us, including the social worker who visited us only once after placement, been more experienced maybe we'd have understood that he needed counseling right from the start, we all did. After all, he'd been born in prison to a heroin-addicted mom and had spent years in and out of foster care.
>
> Mike started sneaking out and creating havoc in the neighborhood. He got into legal trouble. He ran away. It was a never-ending scene of drama, chaos and crisis. At sixteen, he committed a major crime and spent the next two years in a residential treatment center. He never lived with us again. By this time, I felt exhausted dealing with Mike and his many problems. I had neglected my daughters because Mike dominated almost every waking moment. One daughter, Christine, was now in college, the other all but moved in with our neighbors as she couldn't handle the stress when Mike was in the house. I hate to say it, but it was such a relief to be free of the constant turmoil he caused.

Despite all this, my parents went on to become international foster parents, fulfilling their dream of giving back to children from a third-world country. They took in five children from a family from Vietnam. Three permanently and two temporarily. The children were sponsored by Catholic charities but of Buddhist background, further painting our United Nation's portrait. Mom recalls, "The two younger children visited often and were loved like family. Our house was filled with great joy and love, with Danielle, and the three to five foster kids around. Thankfully the foster kids have all become productive, honorable citizens."

Meanwhile, as I was away at college the stories of Mike's troubles came by phone. We largely lost contact, he was in and out of prison and I could not seem to forgive him for his ways. I was angry and wanted no part of his lawless lifestyle. In fact, it only drove me to start volunteering with local law enforcement. As the years went by, my career as a young news reporter/anchor took me from Phoenix, to San Angelo, Texas, to Tucson and finally Los Angeles.

I mentioned earlier that Mike was a great sketch artist, and behind bars he became a sought after tattoo artist working in secret. He also contracted Hepatitis C, and when he got out of prison the disease hit hard. That meant hospital visits would be needed every other day for dialysis to cleanse the blood. I'm guessing Mike would never much follow through with getting the treatments he needed.

Once I was living in L.A., I saw Mike a few times when I'd fly to Tucson to visit Mom. Dad had since passed, died in a tragic scuba diving accident. Danielle had followed Lance to San Diego and they married.

When I'd fly home Mom and I would visit Mike at his apartment or get a quick bite to eat. It was close to the airport for me to fly back to L.A. Sometimes we'd meet at the airport Denny's. During one such visit, I eyed Mike's syrupy pancakes.

"You can have one." He placed one of his pancakes on my plate. It was a loving gesture, but the move meant more to me than a pancake. As we quietly ate our breakfast, the silence screamed of sadness and loss as he looked up at me with those big brown eyes and said,

"I guess I really messed up my life."

"Nah" I said, my eyes looking away masking the lie.

I softly asked why he had gotten into drugs.

"I was sad every day of my life." This broke my heart to hear.

I tenderly asked him, "What role did I play in your life?"

"You showed me what life could be."

Mike died shortly after that at the age of thirty-three of a cocaine overdose.

Despite the hell he brought to my family because of the choices he made, I couldn't help but feel a sadness at how he went out. It was much like how he came into this world, through a mother on drugs, a history behind bars. I couldn't help but feel devastated at the loss. The day he died was a moving moment for my mother and me. Coincidentally, I had gone home to Arizona. It hadn't been too long since my father had died and I would try to get home to be of comfort to Mom. We got the call that Mike had overdosed and were summoned to the hospital two hours away. We were family. We would identify the body. Mom's frantic words echo in my head and tears well up in my eyes as I write this. We rushed through the hospital doors and in a distraught devastated voice Mom called out, "I'm here for my son!"

Her screech echoed in my head. I was silenced. After all the trauma and drama, her wound was exposed. The words hung heavy, "my son."

Years later, the emotion for me is still fresh and raw. Was it any wonder I questioned the system, the process, the concept, adoption itself? Is it any wonder I felt not the man-for-the-job when asked to take on Sunday's Child? Was it any wonder for so many years I refused the title "adoption advocate" and purely preferred non-biased neutral reporter?

It wasn't until recently that I realized all was okay. I was exactly where I was supposed to be.

An Unlikely Adoption Advocate

When I met Jared he was roughly the same age as my brother was when he started doing drugs and our family life changed. I wanted answers as to what went wrong. I wanted to see how our current Wednesday's Child families were making it work. I saw so much love in their eyes, their words, and in their actions, I wondered if my mother and my father had entered the adoption world with equal excitement. If so, what happened—what went wrong? Did they do the best they could at the time? Today, the resources at our fingertips are many. In L.A. County for example there is now mandatory therapy. I wanted to share how our TEAM WC parents are using the resources in building their forever families.

Every child has his history. Jared had one too. County records are confidential, and frankly I'm glad to not officially be in-the-know as to why our children are in foster care. I'm never privy to birth parent background. Still, I've heard enough, however, to know that no child should walk in Jared's little boy shoes. Just as no child should have walked in my brother's shoes. To every person who has ever adopted, including my own parents, I applaud you.

I believe the United States of America has a passionate program, not perfect, but a passionate program to protect children from abuse, neglect and abandonment. It takes a special human being, a special parent to welcome a kid from foster care into their home. They are willing to walk the long walk to success.

I view myself not as an advocate of adoption but as a cheerleader for the children. I pray prospective parents will do their homework. I pray our governments will give our social service agencies and overworked social workers the staffing, training, time and tools desperately needed for them to do the (often thankless) job so many of them love. I pray our children seize the opportunities that do come their way, that they look for the lessons in life and find peace in the journey. I pray for all of our birth families, that a day will come when they put us out of business.

My definition of success has changed over the years. It's not about making straight A's or winning awards, nor is it about a job on TV. I'm no longer waiting for the knight in shining armor or for my fantasy birth father. Success is in the living of life. That means living through the ups and the downs, the valleys and peaks. Each of us will walk a unique walk and each has a gift to offer that is all our own. I've found in the giving you end up receiving. Love is all around us it just sometimes comes in unexpected forms, in unexpected ways and from sometimes the people we least expect.

With more than 500 children adopted over fifteen years, we have a whole lot of Forever Families! It would take volumes to record all of their stories and years to catalog their individual journeys. But it's said that every journey begins with the first step, so what do you say we get started?

I'm honored to share the stories of just a few of the fabulous adoptive families who have crossed my path. Special families who have changed the lives of special children, and in so doing have changed the lives of many others in the process, my own included.

Let's start with the Cates family, for they are living proof of Jared's legacy and have touched me in an equal way.

Dear Chris,

You asked does adoption work? I think you're thinking of the happily ever after concept. In that sense, no, it doesn't. Adoption does "work" as a safe place to grow, make mistakes, to belong and to be loved unconditionally with all of life's challenges. In all of life's challenges, you will win some and you will lose some. Adoptees have a shot at doing this in a place where they won't be rejected.

You yourself didn't stop growing when you became an adult and you will still grow and some of the things you thought you overcame you will vacillate about. Just as our kids will continue to grow and make mistakes, you and I will as well, and the "system" will too. Hopefully with every failure will come a new and better outcome.

Social workers/agencies for decades have been screaming for therapeutic services for all kids as soon as they come into the system to the deaf ears of legislators until the inevitable happened—at detriment to a child, followed by a lawsuit and now at last it's a requirement.

This lawsuit mandating therapeutic services at the onset is known as the Katie A. law. Perhaps if this happened much sooner, Mike would be in a different place? I don't know, but I am so sorry it had not.

Change is gradual but it will happen and good change often requires obstacles and that's why there is no happily ever after, just constantly better ever after, all to each person's uniqueness.

You're not done yet, you will have more challenges and obstacles and you will not always make the right choice but hopefully with life experiences, you, your family and your friends will make better choices and not beat yourself up too badly and surrender completely when you make wrong ones with the support of those who love you.

That's what adoption offers for our kids… not happily ever after, but better ever after and hopefully a safe place to grow and make mistakes.

Respectfully yours,
Will aka: Obi-Wan

Darnell volunteering at National Adoption Day

Chapter 10

My L.A. Family

A razor? I thought in total disbelief. As Darnell continued to pleasantly open his birthday presents I frowned and thought why would anyone give Darnell a razor? When he finished unwrapping his gifts, I whispered to him, "Why in the world would you need a gift like that?" He looked up at me with his soft, beautiful brown eyes and sweetly informed me "I've been shaving for a while now."

Shaving? I could hardly believe my ears. What happened to "our" little boy? Where was little Darnell from Wednesday's Child? Where was that eight-year-old boy in foster care, looking a little forlorn?

I stopped to study him. He'd long-ago been adopted, and I saw indeed "our" little boy was little no more. Standing before me was a handsome, kind, loving, generous, proper, optimistic, educated, mannerly, talented, engaging, sixteen-year-old young man!

He mentioned college and even introduced me to his girlfriend. How could our little guy have grown up so fast? I continued to observe as Darnell basked in the bright lights of his sixteenth birthday bash.

Not having children of my own and seeing Darnell only on occasion, I suppose I never quite understood or remembered what sixteen meant. My own "sweet sixteen" was unmemorable, just another day.

As Darnell's party went on, it was wonderful to watch him and it was indeed a "Dream Day"!

A Red Carpet Birthday

When in Hollywood go Hollywood, and that's what we did for Darnell's bash. Darnell had discovered acting shortly after his adoption, so the theme was a perfect fit. Adoptive mom, Mary, was so into it, running around town picking up the perfect party packages and tinsel town decorations.

As guests arrived for Darnell's big day, they became instant VIPs. We'd lined the walkway with a red carpet and velvet ropes. Darnell's adoptive dad, Arthur, and Will, our program coordinator, played the roles of paparazzi, cameras in hand and flashing.

As for food, we went all out there, too. The one thing Darnell had requested was a chocolate fountain. Mignon Chocolates had long been a friend to Wednesday's Child, so I called in a favor. As guests arrived the fountain awaited. Warm liquid milk-chocolate spilled over the sides as we dipped in our crisp shortbread cookies, sweet strawberries and tart apples.

It was a reunion of sorts with friends from all across town. To break the ice we played a guessing game that had everyone in giggles. Our "celebs" grabbed goofy glasses, bushy feather boas and hip hats to pose for pictures in front of a Hollywood backdrop.

It was a pool party too, and at first only the daring dove in. Eventually, the pool was packed. Darnell wrestled in the water with equally playful and perfectly appropriate teen boys. A backyard barbecue satisfied all the hungry tummies, replete with ribs, hot dogs, and burgers. Some of the guys, growing up ever-so-fast, came back for three and four refills. Mary had borrowed a cotton-candy machine to satisfy the sweet tooth. A popcorn machine made for a salty afternoon snack.

I'd long ago forgotten how much teens can eat, but watching them suddenly reminded me of the times in my childhood when all the neighborhood kids would congregate at our home for backyard pool parties.

Mom was a public school teacher, so our summer vacations from school were also her summer vacations from school. Having always wanted a big family herself, I could now see where including so many kids helped her to achieve that. It wasn't just relegated to our pool, virtually every excursion we went on as kids we'd take as many neighborhood kids and friends as we could pack into the Volkswagen bus. But looking at Darnell and his friends joyfully splashing reminded me specifically of those scorching Arizona summers when our pool was a constant source of refreshment from the sizzling summer heat.

The guests here today were a mix of kids representing Darnell's life. Some from school, others from church, a few more from extra-curricular activities and acting class. He happily reconnected with old friends. One high-tech teen played DJ while a few of the kids mimicked dance moves.

What would any Hollywood event be without speeches, so we incorporated that into the party too. It was my favorite part. We loved and chided Darnell all at the same time. Mom sure let him have it! He took it with grace as Mom showed him no mercy and told his silly secrets. The crowd loved it.

Then it was time for cake, it was designer and delicious, in the shape of an edible iced Hollywood film reel. We sang Happy Birthday to this young man. Aunts, uncles, cousins and Grandma-Nana Pat were there too. Even Darnell's church mentor Mr. Leonard Baker. Darnell's father looked on with pride as we all celebrated his son. He also now had an adopted little brother and sister. It was evident how far we'd come.

Darnell was just eight years old when I'd profiled him on Wednesday's Child.

Arthur and Mary Cates, a married couple with no children were looking to adopt. They met and fell in love with Darnell. They adopted him a year later, he was nine years old.

With most Wednesday's Child families I am lucky if I see them once a year, at our reunion. Like the Thomas', the Cates seemed to keep surfacing. Of the hundreds of families we interact with every year, they were one of the few my newscast had continued to follow, years after the initial foster care segment aired. We'd seen Darnell go from county care to adoption, and at reunions, special events, and now his sixteenth birthday.

This day, however, was different.

Darnell's birthday party was personal. In fact, we held it at my own home, and it had taken a great deal of soul-searching to get here.

This was a landmark day in Darnell's life, and in mine as well.

My House

My friendship with the Cates family had long ago left the office, but was still largely limited to community events together. Things changed one day when I'd offered to drive Darnell home after mom Mary had dropped him off to join me at an event.

On the drive home I had to stop by my house, and seeing it triggered an idea in Darnell.

Wow, this would be a great place to have a party.

He shared the thought with his mom, who later called me with the idea. She gingerly said, "Darnell's birthday is coming up and he thought... maybe your house?"

I had to agree with him. My home at the time was a perfect place for a party. I was blessed to be living in a designer home in the legendary Hollywood Hills and although hardly the size of one, it did have the feel of a mini-mansion. It had three fountains, a big pool, a patio backyard with a cabana, a gourmet kitchen, a bar, plenty of rooms, an open flow, and enough bathrooms.

While largely an unmarried work-aholic with no family in town I'd rarely had a chance to share it with others. For me, my home was investment property, storage, a place to eat, sleep, dress and dash. I'd dreamed of filling it with light and laughter, fun and friendship. A party would be a good excuse to clean, de-clutter and decorate. But was I ready for that?

I was jumping for joy to have been asked, but still a little insecure, I informed her that the thought had indeed crossed my mind too.

Little did Mary know there was huge hesitation in the word that spilled out of my mouth. "Yes."

We decided to talk more about it in the coming few weeks.

This would be a big step for me, and frankly I was petrified, unsure and moved by the emotion of it all.

As a bit of a busy career gal, few people had ever been to my home, only a handful of co-workers, and only one kid ever from Wednesday's Child, my beloved Jared. Losing him was still fresh. Was my heart ready to celebrate another landmark birthday? In my own home no less? Was I ready to know another Wednesday's Child teen, personally as well as professionally?

The idea also begged the question, was I willing to open my door to fifty kids I didn't know? Yet it wasn't just about physically hosting a party, an even bigger battle brewed inside.

Gettin' Personal

Issues rumbled inside as I pondered this birthday party. I was afraid of what it all represented.

My own family was never a celebratory family, not the kind that got together for birthdays, anniversaries, weddings or graduations. Events that might bring other families together were never so for us. We just weren't party people. Career took me in and out of state furthering my isolation and independence. Throughout the years, I'd carried unresolved anger over the loss of my own fairytale fantasy view of family. My adopted brother's dysfunction and drug abuse had frightened me and had literally turned our colorful family into a dark entity. I'd blamed my mom, let my dad off the hook, ran from home. It is unfair to completely throw my parents under the bus, their ways allowed me the freedom to fly away and pursue my dream job.

How could I as a child possibly understand what they were going through? How could I possibly know they were parenting in the best way they thought possible? How could I have asked the questions I now ask and received the comforting answers I now receive? Today, my mother and I are closer than ever.

Yet back then, it made for a lonely journey.

Now, living in Los Angeles and anchoring the 10 p.m. newscast, I was completely engrossed in the obligations of work, activities, friends, the gym, and self-imposed studies. The insecurities of being an anchor in the big-city at the too-tender age of twenty-five gave me a feeling of constant failure as I fought to make the grade. Add to that a series of failed, painful relationships with men, a not too uncommon story in L.A. On the up side there was a constant barrage of exciting invites and activities; however, that too made me not want to miss a weekend to travel back "home." I realize now I also rode the high of finding a fabulous news story, landing an exclusive interview, editing under deadline and airing the perfectly polished news segment. In retrospect, I, too, played a role in walking away from family. As early as high school, Mom reminds me I would say "I can't (go here, go there, help out around the house) because I'm working on my career." At fifteen I got out of doing the dishes by saying "I'm working on my career." Because I always seemed to be "working on my career" I missed out on a lot of fun, turned down stress reducing invitations like lunch with a girlfriend, Thanksgiving at the Naipo's, a cruise with Cristina, a church retreat with Angie, the Beatty's tree trimming party. There was a price to pay.

Isolation turned to loss when my dad drowned in a scuba diving accident, and shortly after, my brother of a drug overdose. Suddenly, almost everyone seemed to be gone. My mom was an only child, so no close aunts, uncles, or cousins. Her parents lived across the country and were nearing ninety. My dad was not close with his out-of-state family. Despite their caring and calls, no relatives, on either side, attended his sudden and unexpected funeral.

Years of therapy played a part in my healing as I worked to recover. Initially opposed to the concept until a best friend, Bennett Williamson, came along and was getting his Ph.D. in psychology. I could no longer make fun of it and Bennett convinced me with this line: "You go to the gym to work out your body, why not therapy to work out your mind?" I always thought of therapy as something for "Beverly Hills women with bad hair days." Ironic that I once lived in Beverly Hills, and with naturally curly hair had no shortage of bad hair days.

As I danced with the idea of a party for Darnell questions still nagged me. Like the Thomas family, the Cates were proof domestic foster care adoption worked, and I liked Darnell, but was I ready to love him? Not the love I gave all the children I encountered, not the love that came from Christine Devine, Fox 11 News anchor. But the love that came from the real me. That girl from back home in Buffalo.

Somehow, I knew opening the door to my home was really opening the door to my heart.

Making the Decision

At the risk of sounding overly dramatic and dismissive of the greater picture of my largely rewarding life, dismissive of all the invites I turned away, all the friends who'd extended invitations that I declined (largely so I could work) I paint this picture.

There's an old movie called, *The Little Match Girl*. In it, there's a scene that has always haunted me. If my memory serves me right, it's a cold snowy night. The starving little girl who tries to earn a pittance selling matchsticks is alone on the empty street. She stands there in despair, her wavy long locks defining her beauty and innocence. She stares longingly into a window watching a large and loving family enjoy a warm, abundant holiday a meal. They pass the rich dishes of turkey, ham, cranberry, mashed potatoes, and yams. There's laughter and love. The fireplace roars. I envision they all held hands in prayer saying grace and giving thanks for the good food. It is all a cozy warmth in which the little girl is denied.

Although I had come a long way in healing, there were still times when I felt like that little girl. Times when I was on the outside looking in.

As crazy as it might sound, that's what Darnell's birthday party represented to me.

Darnell's family would be the warm and wonderful one inside. So picture perfect. With his birthday party I could have just a taste of it. Just a taste of a loving, laughing, intact, active, bonded, friendly family. There'd be abundant food on my table. Laughter, love, joy and warmth. There'd be lots of friends and family and we'd all celebrate!

As we planned the party by phone my mouth said yes but my mind reserved a way out. Mary sensed my trepidation. "Terri and I prayed on it," she later told me. Terri was a close friend. She wasn't sure of the reasons why and just kept on working away. She'd call often with questions. "Should we get colored balloons or gold and silver? Should we hire a food truck or caterer? Should we end the pool party at 5 p.m. or 7 p.m.?"

God-Mom

With the party now about a month away the invitations were being readied. Mary asked to put on the final touch. To my surprise, she asked "should we list you as Auntie... or God-mom?" I was nearly in tears... and petrified all over again! While I knew having the party at my home felt like family, I had no idea they might welcome me as that too. I was overjoyed and flooded with gratitude and emotion.

On that day in August, Darnell's birthday, my home was indeed filled with joy. While the Cates had adopted Darnell, I feel on that day like the Cates adopted the little-kid-in-me too!

My parents were upstanding citizens, ex-foreign aid workers, honored and respected educators, parents who provided leadership and expected responsibility; however, my mom's dream of a big warm loving family just was never to be. Her being an only child hasn't helped. Our tiny little brood is kept together by either Mom, my sister, or me. While that is still the extent of my immediate family, it has become impossible to ignore that I now have a far bigger family in a whole different way than I could have ever imagined. People who have helped me to break down the walls that I had spent years building by much of my own inaction as well as action. People who welcome this little match girl inside their homes, their hearts and their lives.

People like the Cates family, my dream family, and Darnell's *forever family*.

The Cates family at The Freddie Mac Foundation reunion

Chapter 11

My Dream Family—The Cates

The wonderful world of Darnell's family reminds me of the old family-friendly sit-coms you see on TV, like *The Cosby Show*.

Darnell was adopted when he was nine years old. Mary and Arthur Cates are a joyous African-American couple, both wear endless smiles, and exude warm, compassionate and loving spirits. Any child would want to run right into their arms for a great big hug!

While each Wednesday's Child's family has a story as to why they decided to adopt, Mary and Arthur are unique in that they both got a taste of foster care/adoption when they were children. Mary herself was in the system, if only for a short time. When Mary was in the first grade her birth mother fell so ill she had to be hospitalized. Mary explains "my brothers were sent to one foster home and my sister and I spent two weeks in the Purdum's foster home." Her experience was a good one. She remembers "our foster parents were very loving and caring people." When her mom was well enough to leave the hospital the children got to go home. Her story ended like that of many children who enter foster care. They are not in the system permanently and go back with birth parents or relatives if/when life has stabilized.

Arthur's story is much like mine. While never in the system, he never knew his birth-father, and like me he was adopted by his stepfather.

Because of their shared history their understanding of this issue was close and personal. While dating, Mary and Arthur explored their commonality and built on a dream to one day foster, and eventually adopt. Says Mary, "I shared that due to medical concerns, I was unable to have children. Arthur was very compassionate." After marrying they moved forward and decided they'd welcome a baby into their lives by fostering an infant. "We felt that there were lovable children (in the system)," says Mary. "We decided to be a blessing with hopes of giving this child an opportunity to experience a life filled with love, joy and spiritual guidance." They knew they could offer a nurturing family and that safe place to call home.

How to Adopt

Adoption doesn't happen overnight. To learn everything they needed to know about this new exciting territory, the Cates' had enrolled in a county training course. Mary says then "it took approximately two and a half years to complete the home study." Home study means a home evaluation by a social worker. Your neighbors might be interviewed, friends, co-workers. There are background checks and mental evaluations. The Cates' passed. In fact, Mary says "the first social worker was so impressed with our home she'd recommended we by-pass the foster care process and focus on adoption."

Adoption! The Cates were excited and went full-steam ahead building a life for a baby! "We purchased car seats, baby beds, play pens, friends and family gave us high chairs, baby clothes, wipes, and pampers. We had everything we needed for our new baby boy." Mary and Arthur couldn't have been more excited.

What happened next changed everything. It is a reminder that life doesn't always go as planned.

It's no secret that many government agencies have a prolific amount of paperwork to manage. While the Cates readied to become parents, the Department of Children's Services transferred their social worker. All of their home study paperwork got misplaced. Suddenly, everything was on hold.

Some would say it's bad luck, fate, or destiny. People like the Cates might say it was God's plan.

This "glitch" in paperwork changed the course of direction for both the Cates and an eight-year-old boy named, Darnell.

Wednesday's Child

During the time the Cates were dealing with misplaced paperwork, Darnell had already appeared on our recruitment segment. His social workers were actively looking to find him an adoptive family.

The first time we met was at his profile shoot for Wednesday's Child. I found him to be a gentle, good looking little guy with soft brown eyes. Our shoot location was pretty cool, a treat for most any child. It was near the beach at the UCLA Ocean Discovery Center, a marine mammal center with a sea-life petting pool. Looking back as we spoke for this book, Darnell remembers that he actually touched the small sharks as they swam by. He insists, "Miss Christine was afraid to touch the sharks." (I love when he calls me Miss Christine. Arthur and Mary demanded he learn a respect for adults and all adults are addressed with such formality. I chuckle as I still think of myself not as a "Miss" but more like "just one of the kids!")

While the tape from Darnell's shoot is long gone, he remembers a bit of the interview. I often ask the little ones this question "what would you do with a million dollars?" Darnell had stated with confidence, "I want to give kids all the candy in the world."

A TV shoot is sure to stand out for any child. Darnell says he remembers the camera and meeting WC coordinator Will Wong. He says he didn't understand what foster care meant, but did understand why he was no longer with his birth family. His words, "because real family didn't pay attention to me, I was not getting an education, I lived in a bad and abusive environment." In his essay included later in this book, Darnell talks about a gang-banger brother. I'm never privy by law to the reasons children are in foster care. In writing this book, and since Darnell has been adopted, I am only now learning of his life and tough times.

At the shoot, Will noticed that Darnell's clothes were dirty. He recalls it clearly, "Wednesday's Child is about showcasing these kids to prospective parents. We want their first image of the child to be as positive as possible. Plus, their story, look, image and outfit would be on TV and archived for years to come and for families to view."

It was a lesson learned and Will now reminds transporting social workers that this is a big day, the child's big day. He reminds his social workers to inform the foster families and/or make sure the child is dressed and groomed appropriately and is ready for the shoot.

On one occasion a social worker had to stop at a store and buy the child a new sweater because the one he was wearing was tattered and dirty. Meanwhile, other children have arrived in their finest Sunday clothes thanks to a caring foster parent. I still chuckle over the time some little girls arrived in pretty frilly party dresses for a day outside at a playground. I was afraid to get one ounce of sand on their sweet little outfits!

Despite his less-than-perfect attire, and his hair a little overdue for a haircut, Darnell was sweet and likeable. He was just a cute kid, and the camera loved him.

Our shoot ended and the story aired.

It was about a year later before Darnell would come back into my life. Will called with the great news, "Darnell has found a family. He's being adopted!"

But the truth was, a family had found him.

Waiting for Baby

As Darnell was waiting for the right family to surface, the Cates were still waiting for an infant. With their first social worker re-assigned, Mary and Arthur got a new one, Rose. Mary really liked Rose and says, "She came with lots of experience and worked diligently to match us with a baby boy."

One day, the Cates got a call from Rose to attend an upcoming Black Adoption Fair. The purpose of such fairs is to have potential parents meet a number of foster children in a casual, comfortable setting. It's a group event, an informal chance to socialize and explore one another. To some folks on the outside of this adoption experience it might seem a bit odd, but adoption fairs are another recruitment program that, like Wednesday's Child, is about making people aware of the need for adoptive families. In this case it's more specific, as you have adults attending who've already expressed an interest in adoption. For Darnell it was worth it!

Mary was scheduled to be out of town for a business meeting but flew back early to attend. Their adoption process had been years in the making, and they felt certain this was where it would finally happen. Mary recalls, "We attended that adoption fair with the intent of connecting with a baby boy. That's when we met Darnell."

A Change in Plans

While they still had a baby in mind, the Cates enjoyed their day at the Black Adoption Fair meeting children of all ages. In fact, Arthur spent a little time chatting with two siblings. As Mary looked around she noticed the get-acquainted board where photos of all the children in attendance that day were posted.

She was drawn to Darnell's picture. He was eight years old which really didn't fit their game plan, but Mary says "there was something about Darnell's eyes that captured my attention. He was adorable, but his eyes were longing for love and attention."

As Arthur continued to play with the two siblings, Mary decided to wander off and meet Darnell.

"I found him sitting on a bench eating a big hamburger and drinking a can of soda. I asked if the seat next to him was taken and he said yes. I sat down beside him anyway and engaged in conversation. No one came back to reclaim the seat."

They chatted for about ten minutes and then Mary saw Arthur standing a few feet away. As Mary and Arthur started to leave she says "I was approached by Adrienne (Darnell's social worker). She asked if there was anything I would like to know about Darnell, and I took advantage of the opportunity." Mary and Arthur spent the rest of the afternoon with Darnell and his social worker. Mary asked every question thinkable. She suddenly wanted to learn as much as possible about Darnell. There were questions like "how long he had been in foster care, why he was removed from his biological family, where he attended school, his personal challenges and triumphs, etc." Mary liked what she saw. She found Darnell "to be a very inquisitive, sharp and an attractive little boy who was longing to be loved."

I wasn't at all surprised to hear this. At my shoot with this little boy I found Darnell to be just a doll. I'm also not surprised that Mary and Arthur enjoyed him. I am surprised that they would venture so far away from the infant of their dreams. Remember, they already had the baby room all set up at home! Then again, I've met many a parent who saw something in a child that made them do a double-take. Sometimes that trigger is something simple and humorous, other times it's deeply powerful and serious.

As the hours went by, the Cates started seriously pondering a life with Darnell.

"What pushed the idea over the edge that day?" I asked Mary. "Well, it sounds silly now, but both my husband and I are left-handed, when we discovered Darnell was left-handed, we were sold!"

As they left the adoption fair the Cates could hardly contain themselves. They called their own social worker from the car, practically shouting with joy, "We have great news! We fell in love and found our baby boy, his name is Darnell."

Getting to Know Each Other

With plans for a baby now replaced by plans for a little boy, the Cates returned the crib, car seat, clothes and playpen. They were moving full-steam ahead with Darnell. The next step was a visitation.

The Cates would see Darnell for the first time since the adoption fair. All sides agreed to meet at a kid-friendly place, Shakey's Pizza. Mary says "Darnell was surprised to see us, but he remembered us, he even remembered our names."

Darnell remembers that day well. I asked him to reflect back and tell me what he initially thought of these strangers who would later become Mom and Dad. "I felt comfortable and my dad was tall like Shaq (NBA basketball). My mom had eyes like (actress) Regina King." The three enjoyed the cheesy pizza and laughed over the arcade games. Before leaving the restaurant Arthur gave Darnell a small gift, a matchbox car.

As I write that last line I tear up. It once again brought back the memory when my family went to the animal park with Mike. Like Darnell, Mike was eight, too.

That first meeting was convincing for Mary and Arthur. Mary says "as we drove away, we watched Darnell as he watched us leave. I wanted to take him with us." Their next visit would be at the Cates' family home.

First Home Visit

The schedule was all set for the first family outing. Arthur would pick Darnell up from his foster home on a Saturday morning and take him back that same night. On the way to the Cates' there was an unnerving incident.

Mary explains, "Darnell surprised my husband when he insisted that he knew how to get to his biological family's house. The bigger surprise came when they drove past Darnell's grandmother's apartment and she and his aunt were out on the porch. Darnell recognized his grandma and she recognized him." Arthur continued driving and the two made their way to the Cates' home.

As Mary opened the door she remembers Darnell was in dirty clothes and wearing shoes that were too big for him. She says "My attempt to wash his clothes was to no avail." If you recall, Darnell arrived much the same for his Wednesday's Child shoot. Not the best reflection of that foster home, sad to say.

Overall, it was a really nice first day at home for everyone. Mary says "We had a great time together. Darnell met the neighborhood kids, and played with our dog." Later that day they'd meet some of Mary and Arthur's relatives.

"We talked to Darnell about joining our family." His response was that he explained he needed to find a new place to live because there were too many boys where he was living and his foster mother told him he had to leave because he was eight years old. Mary had clearly been moved. She says "saddened by Darnell's comments, I immediately asked him if he would like to come and live with the Cates family."

"Yes!" Darnell smiled. Two months after their first meeting, he moved in with the Cates.

In Darnell's Words

"I felt like I was at home the very first time I came to visit.

"When I would go from foster home to foster home, the people would be mostly nice to me, but at night I was scared and I would break out in a sweat and I could not sleep.

"When I came to my new parents' home, I felt comfortable at the very beginning and I could sleep at night. I came in and ran to find and play with my new dog, Kasji. I knew this was the right home and the right parents for me."

Adjusting

Every family will have a different story about the adjustment period. For the Cates' it "was fairly smooth" says Mary. Her job allowed her to telecommute so she was home for Darnell and able to "bond relatively quickly."

Other families may tell a different story, paint a different picture. Be reminded how tough it might be for the children. New faces, new location, new school. While adoption for parents can be a happy thing, it is important to keep in mind that these children have experienced trauma which led them to being in foster care in the first place. Darnell says the hardest part were the "new responsibilities, new rules." Parents are wise to also understand that a child might experience a mix of emotions.

For the Cates' one challenge early on was to find the right school for Darnell. He was behind several grades and catching up was important in so many ways. Mary says "ultimately, we enrolled him in a Montessori school with great teachers who were willing to work overtime to help him get to grade level."

There was another issue at play here, one that had left a wound. Mary says Darnell had been bullied both in his foster home and at his elementary school. "Because of this, he was guarded and had difficulty making new friends." She adds "when I was out of town on business trips, Darnell's behavior would decline and it would improve when I returned home."

Mary put extra effort to "ensure Darnell fully understood that he was loved and wanted." She would "leave notes on the bathroom mirror, in his backpack reminding him how much we loved him and wanted him to be a part of the family." A unique and loving gesture, "I would spell his name with alphabet blocks as Darnell Cates and leave them on the living room floor for Darnell to find. We spoke in detail about adoption day to make sure Darnell was comfortable and that he understood he would not have to move to another home."

Still it would take another month-or-so for it to start to feel like family. Christmas was approaching and Mary attempted to get Darnell to make a wish list. "This was very difficult for Darnell. He made excuses, he made disrespectful comments and for the first time since he'd moved in with us Darnell even talked about going back to his foster family." Mary asked Darnell "to go and sit in the den and think about why he wanted to be a part of our family." When she checked on Darnell she saw him crying. It was a first. He cried "I thought you said you loved me." Mary says "We made up, and together we wrote the letter to Santa. We watched movies together that night and he lay in my arms as if he were my natural son."

The bond continued to build. Another poignant moment "I recall our first trip to Universal City together. Darnell sat on Arthur's shoulders to watch the parade." It was a father son moment and very real. The Cates had a wonderful first Christmas. Mary describes it as "full of fun and surprises, our first Christmas as a family."

Adoption

As for the adoption process itself, again, every family will have their own story and feelings about the process. Again, for the Cates' this part too went smoothly. Mary says "we had great social workers and a great group of attorneys at the Alliance For Children's Rights working on our behalf. Birth parental rights were terminated and there were no roadblocks."

To give you an idea of the length of time it takes to adopt once child and parent meet keep this in mind. The Cates met Darnell in September. He moved to the home in November. An adoption date was set in May. The adoption would happen in August. Coincidentally, it was set for August 2, Darnell's ninth birthday. That sounded perfect to the Cates! They sent out adoption notices to friends and family.

Celebrate

On his ninth birthday Darnell was adopted. Yes, it was a day of celebration! Friends and family attended as well as cameras and news media.

Mary looks back on that day as "a day we will always remember. The adoption solidified our family union." The entire Cates entourage celebrated with a birthday party at Chuck E. Cheese.

Mary notes there is a side-bar reason to remember this day fondly. "As a result of our adoption, our friends Deidra and James decided to adopt a child in the county foster care system." While officially we count more than 500 adoptions, we take pride in the spin-off effect. I was once honored at an adoption event and the speaker credited WC with thousands of adoptions. I was stunned. Could the spill-over be that wide spread?

Even the Cates would go on to adopt two more outside of the Wednesday's Child program. Darnell would get a little brother and sister, Phillip and Sierra. But first, let's get Darnell settled.

Family Forever

The Cates' home is as lovely as they are. It is in a well-groomed middle class neighborhood. Friends live just across the street. It feels like Mayberry. It feels perfect. It feels like a home for a family, a safe, peaceful place for a child to call home.

Adoption, however, never means happily ever after. It means "the next chapter in life." I asked Mom, Mary, to be honest about some of the struggles. With Darnell's permission she shared realities, lessons learned, parenting skills put to the test.

Mary says, "Overall, Darnell is a good son. He has a compassionate heart and will reach out to help anyone." That's the core of Darnell. Still, as much as we all love him, we too know Darnell is a growing human being like all of us. He's lived life with a birth family and then foster families and now an adoptive home. He came to the Cates with some preconceived notions, patterns, teachings, behaviors and beliefs. It takes time, compassion, patience, and love, to build a forever family.

Life Lessons

For starters says Mary "I'm not sure if it was due to rejection or a built-in survival mechanism, but Darnell would make up stories and he was believable at eight years old. He told his second grade teacher that he grew up in the jungles of China and played with jungle animals. He convinced my husband that he and his grandmother took a trip to New York and he visited the Statue of Liberty. He provided enough details about the Statue of Liberty to make you believe the trip was real, but in reality, Darnell had never been out of the state of California. We worked with Darnell to help him understand the importance of telling the truth."

Lesson number two. "We're told Darnell's birth brother, the gang member, taught him to steal from the local liquor store," Mary adds. "So he would take things from the grocery store and from us just because he wanted too." Mary tells a great story of their little boy discovering Dad's valuable coin collection and thinking it would make for some easy pocket change.

The couple worked hard breaking Darnell of such beliefs. "We worked with Darnell to help him understand the importance of not taking things that belong to others. It took a lot of time and a lot of prayer, patience, time-outs and eventually, I began taking away the things he loved to play with until the habit was broken."

The Cates began setting healthy boundaries for Darnell.

Let's remember that life lessons like this don't come just with children who've been in the system. I refrain from painting them as "bad kids." In fact, the Darnell stealing story reminded me of an incident from my own childhood.

One time when I was a little girl I grabbed a small handful of colorful two-cent beads from a gift shop. Yellows, blues, reds. They were such pretty colors. Later, my mom found them in the laundry. She instantly grabbed my hand and put me in the car, drove right up to the shop and made me apologize. I was a little girl and remembered thinking "lady, they're only two-cent beads." Still, my mom knew the importance of teaching me not to steal early on. To this day I thank her for the lesson. To this day I am mortified and can still see the vision of me apologizing in that store and can still see that great big basket of beautiful beads.

Darnell had to overcome a negative belief-system, including some experiences that had scarred him. He remembers feeling cheated when his foster family would go out to eat. He says their birth son would get two cheeseburgers and he'd ponder "how come I only got one." He remembers at Christmas getting little, nothing but a box of cookies. That was his only gift. He learned at a young age that he was unworthy, unwanted, and for the most part, unwelcome.

Perhaps scarred in his own way, my adopted brother would hide and hoard food under his bed. My mom could never understand it as there was plenty of food for us all.

About his adoptive family, Darnell gets back to the basics. "I get fed well, they buy me clothes and things, not just getting a cheeseburger."

Patient Parenting

What works? Mary says she reflects on her own childhood to stay grounded. She admits it can be a challenge as with any child.

Mary credits open communication for their healthy family relationship. She says "we love Darnell as our own son. Darnell and I truly bonded as mother and son. We can talk about anything. He is not afraid to ask the tough and embarrassing questions." Mary makes clear "Yes, at times he can be challenging and yes, at times I wonder if he really understands how much we love him."

The Cates' are blessed in that they have the nearby support of family. They also find strength in their commitment to church and God. Faithful Central is one of L.A.'s large and strong churches. Mary says, "in tough times, we talk, we pray, I talk to friends who are raising children or have gone through similar struggles." Darnell too finds peace in their Christian faith. I asked what he's learned from his family. He says, "I can do anything if I put my mind to it. I learned about God."

The Cates have fully invested in Darnell's interests and encouraged extra-curricular activities of his choice. Both made the time to fully be present and participate. Despite Mary's concern as to whether he truly knows he's loved, Darnell assures me otherwise. "They love me and take me places where I need to go, they support me."

Adopting Again

With Darnell working out so well, Mary and Arthur decided to adopt again. Adding more children to the mix added its own issues. Sibling rivalry proved to be an opportunity for more life lessons and challenged Darnell in a whole new way. Darnell had wanted a sister but ended up with a sister and a brother.

It was a chance encounter that led to the adoption of Sierra and Phillip. The two sides met at a radio station during a promotion for the adoption of older children. As they sat in the lobby, Mary says a little girl came over and started to play with Darnell. "Although this little girl did not talk much, she and Darnell played together very well." Seems that was all it took for Darnell. Mary says he "looked at me and said, Mom, maybe she could be my little sister." Mary learned the girl had a brother. "She pointed to a little boy sitting in the social worker's lap. This little boy was full of energy." Mary asked all the important questions of the sibling's social worker. She then called her own social worker, Rose.

As a family, the Cates' decided to take the next step. They'd meet the children. For Sierra and Phillip, the future was uncertain. They were living in a group home that was about to close and the children would most likely be placed in different foster homes away from one another. Mary was moved. "I could not bear the thought of Phillip and Sierra being separated." She and Arthur agreed to take both children.

L.A. County attempts to keep children together, however it doesn't always work out that way. I have one teen who preferred not to be adopted by the same couple adopting her little brother. We're still searching for the right fit for her. Often times you'll find families willing and able to offer a home to one or two children but not a large sibling group. Other times you have families looking for a certain age and that child comes with siblings much older or much younger.

The Cates were like many other families I've seen. They wanted a sister for Darnell, were sold on Sierra, and stepped up to include baby brother.

Home Sweet Home

Mary says their first weekend felt like family. It was just a visit but still Mary says something magical happened.

"Phillip is an animated child. We were all in the back yard playing and Phillip yelled to Arthur. . . "What ya doing Dad?" We all stopped to stare and Darnell asked, "Hey guys, did you hear what Phillip said?"

Phillip and Sierra moved in shortly afterwards and the bonding process began. "They began to learn their new address and home and to spell Mommy and Daddy's names," Mary said.

One look at Phillip and you're sure to agree he is completely adorable. His happy toothy grin is captivating. His bouncy energy is infectious. Mary describes Phillip as a loveable child but notes "his struggles were different. He was very anxious, moving a mile a minute (so it seems). He was five years old when he joined our family, yet he could not hold a pencil or write his name. He did not know how to read, nor did he know the alphabet."

Mary says Sierra was also behind. "Sierra was and still is very shy. She was tongue-tied and could not speak clearly. She had problems writing her name. She would act out in school to divert attention away from the fact that she was seven years old and in kindergarten."

The Cates' secured resources for Sierra and feel she is making progress. They note Phillip was able to catch up to age level and skipped kindergarten.

Their adoption took place on July 27, 2007, two years after meeting. Their kindergarten teacher and classmates attended the adoption. L.A.'s famed Judge Michael Nash presided, just as he had on Darnell's day. Judge Nash is considered to be the father of our nation's National Adoption Day.

Happy Home

With three kids in the house parenting took on added importance. Mary's job had her working ten hour days and traveling an hour or two just to get there. That left only the weekend or time in the car for bonding with the kids.

"Arthur and I discussed it at length and agreed that a major change needed to occur, and so I retired early so I could be home with the children."

Mary takes great pride in parenting and enjoys bringing to life things she didn't have growing up. "There are many things that

I longed for when I was a child." She describes her own mother as very strict and overly protective. "Because of that, I missed out on the opportunity to socialize with kids in the neighborhood, and to attend school functions. It makes me happy to see Darnell interacting with other children, participating in school and church activities, being a leader in the neighborhood, and a big brother to Phillip and Sierra."

Surrounded in Happiness

"Family time is my favorite time, and we have a lot of it," Mary said. "It makes me happy when all of the kids come and crawl into bed with me and together we watch a family movie. It makes me happy to see Sierra pick up a book and read a story, write her name, teach herself how to ride her bike and skate. It makes me happy to hear her acknowledge her brother's accomplishments. It makes me happy to watch her grow into a beautiful little girl. It makes me happy to watch Sierra and Phillip play together without fighting. It makes me happy to watch Phillip write his name. It makes me happy to watch him in acting class, he is so adorable! It makes me happy to watch Phillip play with other children without fighting or demanding his way. It makes me happy to watch him tie his shoes.

"And I'm convinced that Darnell can succeed at whatever he sets his mind to do, and when I look at him, it makes me happy to know that he is happy. Society had deemed Darnell as unadoptable. It makes me happy to know that with the help of God, we have made a positive impact on his life, perhaps saved his life."

Adjusting All Over Again

"At the end of the day, what keeps our family together is love." Mary insists that is the glue that bonds them through the good and the bad. Because, yes, there were tough times ahead with the new adoptions. With three Cates kids, Darnell was now a big brother, which also meant sharing a bedroom. More important than that, it also meant Darnell had to make very different choices in how he related to his new siblings.

This was a serious concern for Mary and Arthur early on.

"Darnell developed a love/hate relationship with Phillip and attempted to do some of the hurtful things his own birth brother did to him. When Darnell was with his dysfunctional birth family, there was very little parenting going on. He needed to learn that he could not get away with this behavior because we would not tolerate it."

There is a much-recited poem by Robert Fulghum that declares *All I Really Need to Know I Learned in Kindergarten.*

While that may be true for many, when it comes to some of the kids caught up in the foster care system, a great deal of what they learned while growing up needs to be un-learned. Things like; parents can't be trusted, nothing is permanent, it's okay to hit, and love hurts.

Darnell confirmed to me that learning to protect and love his adopted little brother came with a lot of internal soul searching and hard work. My advice to him was to continue seeking the support of his family and church as he sought answers to the challenge of not only living together, but loving one another.

The good news here is that the parents persevered, the church mentors made sure to keep a watch, and Darnell kept an open heart and mind. Phillip himself eventually won over big brother. Mary says, "Even though Darnell would do things to try and hurt Phillip or get him in trouble, Phillip would still follow him around like a puppy, Phillip loved him. Darnell quickly learned to get along with Phillip. Today, they are the best of brothers."

The story with Sierra was a little different. Mary says, "To Darnell's surprise, having a little sister was more than he bargained for. She does not allow Darnell to boss her around." Mary confirms there is a healthy sibling relationship now and they are indeed a family experiencing sibling rivalry at its best! "My long-term dream for Sierra is that her brothers always watch out for her and protect her."

Mary seems to relish every mom moment. Whenever we talk she seems to be running one kid or another to some kind of practice, party, or acting audition. Acting classes for both boys also keep the calendar full. Phillip is in Little League, and Sierra is into dance and modeling.

> "Wednesday's Child is the Golden Stork that brings amazing little blessings to their Forever Families."
>
> Arshia, WC viewer

Watching the Cates family grow together, and being embraced by them myself, has been therapeutic for me. It's helped me better understand why I was so petrified to be anything but a neutral and unbiased reporter during my early years on this assignment. This kind of family interaction was a faded memory for me. I was out of my comfort zone. Much like Darnell, I had to unlearn belief systems that were second nature to me. Such as, domestic adoption doesn't work.

Because I've learned that is simply not true.

Growing with God

The Cates are quick to say they did not do all of this alone. In fact, their story really is one that exemplifies the concept posed by First Lady Hillary Clinton, that it "takes a village."

Faith is an important part of the Cates' family life, and they turned to their church family for help in raising their boy.

"We enrolled Darnell in the Faithful Central Bible Church 'Rites of Passage Program' which reinforced the training we provide in the home," Mary said.

I had the pleasure of attending Darnell's graduation ceremony for this leadership program. When I arrived I found a huge crowd of family and friends and a large stage. How polished the boys all looked in their "uniforms." All stood tall and confident. Their assigned adult male mentors stood nearby. All of these boys were polite and well mannered. All were open to the leadership, love, tough talk and spiritual teachings. Parents applauded. Parents were present. The men of the church stood in commitment to help raise these boys. Darnell indeed had family. Mom, Dad, sister Sierra and brother Phillip all sat in the audience and watched attentively.

Mary was on a mission. "My ultimate desire for both Darnell and Phillip is that they make sound choices and develop healthy acquaintances, avoid negative influences and live as law abiding and faith-filled young men," she says. "His dad and I gave Darnell a Scripture passage at his Right Of Passage Graduation that we hope will carry him into his adult life. It speaks to the importance of the Bible itself, it comes from Joshua 1:8."

> *Keep this Book of the Law always on your lips; meditate on it day and night, so that you may be careful to do everything written in it. Then you will be prosperous and successful.*
>
> Joshua 1:8 New International Version

I knew between the Cates' and church Darnell had a fighting chance. With the alarming number of young black men in gangs or prison, I knew Darnell was being positioned to be a success story. Mary and Arthur have a purpose. "We want to make a difference in how they view family, with the hope that one day they will marry and raise families of their own and have the opportunity to pour good Christian values and morals into their children's lives. My long-term goals for each of our kids is that they love God and have a personal relationship with Him," Mary remarked.

At his graduation, Darnell was voted "Overall Excellent Achiever." I beamed with pride, right along with his parents. Most improved to me meant he was open to the guidance and love others so wanted to give. Darnell had become a conscientious young man. He had mentors who were more than willing to hold him accountable. He wasn't alone in his journey.

For several years I kept their leadership guidelines posted on my wall at work. This family is my inspiration and role model.

Sixteen

At sixteen, Darnell continues to grow into himself. He is a dynamic and dedicated high school student. The kid wakes up at 5:30 in the morning to board the city bus to his college-prep campus. Darnell was accepted into one of the finest Fine Arts schools in the nation. A perfect place for him to pursue his acting. Although he tells me Algebra is his favorite class!

As for the acting, Darnell is currently represented across the board by The Savage Agency which is one of L.A.'s Top talent agencies for kids and teens and he has already starred in an award winning short film entitled *A Blind Man*. He has held starring and/ or leading roles in eight more short films within a one year period. He has appeared in two commercials and on Nickelodeon and Cartoon Network Game shows.

"He's a natural and believable actor and he is very passionate about his work. I dream of sitting in the audience at the Oscars one day, tears of joy messing up my make-up and watching him receive awards for what he loves best. But I've assured him that he is loved whether he is acting or not," Mary said.

While an acting career is developing, Mary informs me Darnell has also expressed interest in being a journalist for *National Geographic Magazine* or a talk show host or screenplay writer. It's good to know he is exploring his many options.

Darnell's acting shots

Mary is the all-supportive mom cartin' the kid around to every audition. Phillip is following in big brother's footsteps appearing in two national commercials, a NIKE ad being one of them. She says "Sierra wants to be a teacher and a mommy like me. They are still young enough to change their minds."

For the Cates family school is a priority with college in mind. Mary says their goal as parents is for the children to "matriculate into society with the ability to be successful in whatever they set their minds to do." Darnell's grandmother, Nana, has dangled a tasty carrot before his eyes to further encourage him, as she's promised to give him her Porsche when he graduates college!

Knowing how important faith is to the Cates family, I asked Mary to share one of her favorite passages, and perhaps some closing words of wisdom.

"I would be lying if I said the adoption journey was easy, because it wasn't. Would we do it again? Absolutely. But I'm not sure I would have made it without leaning on God. There were countless times when I had no idea what I was going to do next, but I always knew where to turn. A source of strength for me is the Bible, and Isaiah 41:10 became my go-to verse many times."

So do not fear, for I am with you; do not be dismayed, for I am your God. I will strengthen you and help you; I will uphold you with my righteous right hand.

Isaiah 41:10 NIV

Insight

You might say I've gotten to watch the Cates family grow-up. First meeting Darnell, then the adoption, the reunion party, the added siblings, more reunion parties and now Darnell's teenage years. We've decided to wait until Darnell turns eighteen for the next big birthday bash, and until then, we'll all carry memories of his sixteenth birthday for a long time. It was so great to see our guy enjoy his day. For that day, I had a great big family. The love, fun and friendship was palpable.

> "Wednesday's Child may be the reason a child one day becomes our future President and has more compassion, resourcefulness, creativity and vision for the future of our country."
>
> Rose, WC Viewer

Happy Birthday to Me

I largely ignore my birthday every year due to the fact that it comes at the start of a busy and crucial ratings month in the news business and often falls on election day, a very demanding day in my business.

My last birthday, Mary asked to drop by my office with a little something. Generally, it's almost impossible to make time for friends and family on that day as my energy is all about ad-libbing election results. It really is a crazy time in virtually every

TV station around the country. But this was the Cates family, and I made an exception.

Mary, Darnell and baby brother Phillip popped by the station, arriving just two hours before air time. Darnell waltzed in with a bunch of balloons in hand. Mary carried a bright yellow box with a petite pink cake inside. There was a present too. I unwrapped a large angel perfect for my house. We wolfed down small slices of the delicious lemony cake, and it touched me they had remembered that lemon is my favorite. It was a sweet distraction from the stress of early election returns.

After they left, I pondered the interruption and allowed myself the human moment of celebrating a birthday and the kindness in their effort. I glanced again at the birthday card Darnell had given me, "To my God-Mommy."

While initially frightened and unsure of letting my work with Wednesday's Child spill over into my home or office, I came to realize that it was no big deal, as my work had already spilled over into my heart.

And that was a very good thing.

Although there were a lot of winners on that election night, I think I held the greatest victory of all.

The Diaz family at our Six Flags Magic Mountain reunion

Chapter 12

Our First Foundation Family—The Diaz Family

You might call the Diaz family our "First Family." They were the first family the Freddie Mac Foundation chose to highlight when L.A.'s long running Sunday's Child program was merged with their national Wednesday's Child program. Our new partnership was announced at a celebratory luncheon where we learned of this new adoption. The three Diaz siblings had appeared on Sunday's Child and we were thrilled to learn they'd found a forever family. It was at this luncheon where I would meet the Diaz parents.

Until we became Wednesday's Child we did little tracking. It was the start of us following families, learning of adoptions, sharing the good news. It was the start of us answering a question I often got from our viewers "Whatever happens to the kids? Do they ever get adopted?" When we met they were young kids, Latino, no older than twelve. For our shoot we went to the race track, behind the scenes at the stables. I was ecstatic to learn they were out of the system.

Parents Richard and Sandra are a loving Latino couple with no children of their own. Both had grown up with lots of family and had imagined they'd have the same. I always find it a tall order to take in siblings.

> "I truly admire you, I wish you were around when I was younger and in Foster Homes and Group Homes."
>
> Eli, WC viewer

But here you have the example of people wanting to fill their homes with lots of children.

I got to know the Diaz family as they too never went away, they attend every reunion and it is always a joy to see them. Mom Sandra always wore a warm smile and offered a great big comforting hug. Dad Richard was the ever-present doting father. Austin was the big brother and always the leader of the pack. Gary was sure to be shy, possessing a sweet innocence. Bianca is the sister and always gave me a look of love and adoration. All were open to television interviews and mom Sandra never failed to spill tears of joy. More than once she has exclaimed "you gave me my family. Wednesday's Child gave me my family."

As time went on the Diaz family came to be a featured follow-up family. Once, we went to their home to cover an at-home example. I was amazed by all of the cousins the kids now had and how they enjoyed a game of pick-up basketball in the front yard. Bianca showed off her bedroom with pride. This is exactly what Wednesday's Child was all about. A safe, permanent place to call home. It was a far cry from the trauma that led these children in to foster care. Austin will tell you how they were on the streets, living in a car. He'll tell you of bouncing from foster home to foster home.

While I hate to portray foster homes as evil and ugly, each child will have their own memory. Some bitter, some sweet, and all leaving lasting impressions on the hearts of the kids. Some kids will tell me they want an adoptive family just like their foster family. Mary Cates decided to adopt because she had such a positive experience when she was in foster care herself. Our foster families are a vital piece of the puzzle and I'm most

> "When I was a child moving from home to home... I missed my bed, my parents and the desire to feel needed. Each home I moved from brought a sense of doubt and thoughts of did I really matter to anyone."
>
> Pamela, WC viewer

amazed by the foster families that take in dozens and dozens of kids.

My parents had opened our home to five. While only living with us a short time, my foster sister B.T. (Terrisa Lynn Nguyen) is now among my closest confidants, best friends, forever family. We were soul mates from day one despite a ten year age difference. I was in college and came home for the summer. B.T. was eleven years old and would follow me all around the house. I'd not seen someone ever look at me with such admiration and awe. While B.T. went on to live in a number of foster homes we never lost touch and today I fly her from Arizona to California each year for a Hollywood-style get-away. Sometimes I feel a mama role, other times I wonder who is really older. B.T. is wise beyond her years, confident beyond belief and physically a knock-out. I am silenced and awestruck knowing such a bond could have come this way. Still, bottom line, foster care isn't a permanent environment, and going from home to home even in the best of circumstances can be traumatizing for any child. Even B.T. will tell you stories. They are stories that sadden my heart yet also encourage the fight for these children.

Our second follow-up with the Diaz clan was another success story. Austin was graduating from high school. While I'm sure other children who'd appeared on our channel had reached this milestone, Austin was the only one we knew of. So, for us, this was huge!

Our first kid to graduate from high school. A landmark.

We arrived with the Fox 11 news camera in hand and Austin was quite the star amongst his classmates. It was wonderful to see this young man beam with pride and wear his green graduation uniform with confidence. Yet it got even better, as Austin was continuing on to college with a scholarship in music. Austin says the high school marching band helped give him a focus from a kid who could have gone astray to one with direction, meaning and leadership. He is quick to credit Wednesday's Child with saving him from an uncertain life, and although his journey has lately taken some twists and turns, he is still one of our key spokesmen.

Brother Gary also attended some college and is now a home-care worker. Bianca is still in high school.

Sandra and Richard Diaz are an example of our families who can't get enough. They went on to adopt three more siblings, and if anyone is willing to build them a bigger house, they will adopt more! In fact, they've already applied. They are an example of the spill-over effect of Wednesday's Child, families adopting children beyond our program.

Recently, I asked Richard Diaz a few questions about his take on the experience of domestic adoption within the foster care system. Beginning with why did he and Sandra want to adopt children in the first place, especially those in county foster care?

> When my wife and I first met, we talked about our plans for the future and whether they included kids. We both agreed there were way too many needy kids in the world and we both knew that we wanted to adopt. At the time, we thought we would have a biological child and adopt a child.

How did you come to meet the children you adopted?

> We attended the MAPP workshop and the adoption workshop. MAPP stands for Model Approach to Partnerships in Parenting... (a "states required pre-adoption course.") One thing that stuck in our heads was that the county would help to financially subsidize the adoption. The main reason we decided on having only one child was because we knew we could not afford any more and still live within our means.
>
> When the realization of financial assistance came up, we sat down and decided that we both came from big families and we truly wanted a large family, so if the county would help us to realize this dream, then why not?

> That is not to say that folks should do this for the money. It's not that much, but with a lot of love and patience it will help you scrape by. As far as our kids, we saw them on an episode of Wednesday's Child. My wife looked at me and I looked at her and she said, 'Call them, we have nothing to lose.' We called and then we prayed and prayed and prayed. Then, we got the call that we could meet them.

Richard's response caused me to remember a challenge within my own family. At that time, there was no government financial assistance for families who adopted. That meant my father's sole salary as a principal needed to support five of us. Money was so tight my parents would sacrifice wherever they could, and would often wear old clothes. For families with their own child keep in mind it is a big change for them too. Not only does it mean sharing mom and dad, it might mean sharing a bedroom, toys, time and activities.

I think the message here is that adopting is a life changer. There are pros and cons and very real issues, choices and sacrifices. Families now receive financial assistance when they adopt, so money troubles should be less of a matter. Does it mean financial concerns are over? No. But there is help and it can make a difference.

I asked Richard to tell me about the adjustment period.

> The adjustment period was at times very difficult. It still is. We first met them at a park. Crazy as it sounds, we immediately fell in love. The older child was very outgoing and so was the younger one (she was a little chatty Kathy). The middle child however was very shy and withdrawn. Still is, to a point. At the time we lived about forty-five miles away and had to come and visit them (very small price to pay). After about six visits, we had a sleep over. We went out for dinner,

came home, watched movies, made popcorn, watched more movies and just stayed close to each other. The next day we went outside and played. Nothing elaborate. We really had a good bonding time. On the third sleepover, they stayed."

I think it was very hard on the kids, they were uprooted again, with a new family, new school, new friends. Eventually, I think what got them through it was the fact that they knew it was the last time.

When did you and Sandra realize they were part of the family? When did they realize this was home?

I think when we first met them, we knew we would be a family. Like I said, I know that sounds crazy, but we actually knew in our hearts it was meant to be. As far as the kids, that was a different story. I think they wanted it to be home but history had proven otherwise. They had been uprooted so many times, it was hard for them to trust that this would be the last time. We had our ups and downs and believe me, a lot more downs than ups at first, but the ups were really up, and that kept us going. Those kids did not stop testing us until adoption day. Yes it was tough. Would we do it again? In a heartbeat.

Tell me about adoption. What was it like for you? For your children?

To be honest, I felt that adoption day was more for the kids. I mean, we were excited, but in our hearts we were already a family. It took the judge telling my kids they were ours, for them to finally believe it. That piece of paper meant a lot to them.

We all know children aren't always easy. So be real. Share some of the struggles.

> Oh my gosh, were there struggles. We adopted a sibling set of three and the oldest was already ten years old, with a personality all his own. He had been through a lot and remembered it all. Social Workers do the best they can, but they don't always tell you everything, and they don't always know everything to begin with.
>
> Because our kids were moved around a lot, they were all behind in school, so they acted out a lot. Our middle son, we found out, had a habit of hiding under the bed. You could just imagine our shock when we couldn't find him. Boy, he really scared us. Our daughter only spoke Spanish (which I don't).
>
> The first couple of years were so hard. But the first time they call you 'Dad,' when they bring home a paper from school and they are so proud, it makes it all worth it. When you are walking and they put their hand in yours, nothing in this world can compete with that.

So, how do you make it work? Where do you turn in tough times? What keeps the family together?

> We're just like any family, we just do it. You take the good with the bad. You concentrate on the good and let the bad just float off your back. I think every town has a post adoption group, if you are having tough times, you can seek their guidance. You are not alone. As far as keeping the family together? Before you adopt, you really have to be committed to the adoption. You have to realize that no child is perfect and if you are looking for that perfect child then just forget adoption. It is not going to happen.

What are your goals for your children?

> Our goal is that whatever they do they are happy doing it. Expect the very best but accept what they have to offer. Realize your child's limitations, but don't limit your child.

When you look at them what makes you the happiest? How have you seen them excel?

> It may sound corny, but just looking at them makes me happy. As far as them excelling, my boys excel in music and my daughter in math. It seems that all other classes are hard and they really struggle, but when they play their instruments or when she is doing math problems, everything seems to be at peace.

What are your long-term dreams for your children?

> I think that goes along with the previous question. I do not expect my children to be doctors or lawyers, I just want them to excel in what makes them happy. My dream is to see them happy.

The Diaz family is already looking into adopting another sibling group. Sandra smiles and says "that's what we do."

When I first met this wonderful couple they assured me they always wanted a big family. Question now is, how big will it get? The book is still open on this one, the chapter not yet written. It is families like them that have also helped me appreciate the realities of adoption. Despite any and all challenges they continue to adopt through foster care.

They may be Wednesday's Child's "First Family," but thankfully, they are not the last.

Some of Our Wednesday's Child Forever Families

The Abbotts, The Bennets, The Brocks, The Jaramillos,
The Cates, The Clivers, The Cottons, The Diazs,
The Elys, The Bransons, The Felders, The Glynns,
The Hollensteiners, The Garcias, The Perskys,
The Newtons, The Sandovals, The Scarfs,
The Doyle-Embreys, The Johnsons,
The Silcocks/Ann Belles, The Cassells
and The Williams.
So many more deserving of a shout out!
You are in our hearts.

Abby, Rob, Madison, Austin and Joey at home

Chapter 13

The Instant Family—The Smith Family

Abby and Rob were a married couple who both worked in the entertainment business behind the scenes. They envisioned having a family. They'd wanted one of their own and planned to adopt another. Abby had grown up with cousins who'd been adopted so it was familiar territory. She'd also known three families who'd adopted children in county foster care and knew the children to be "wonderful."

But the first goal didn't go as planned. Perhaps it rarely does. Abby and Rob were unable to conceive. Hopes of bringing home a baby from the hospital were not to be, without a little help. Abby says they "briefly looked into fertility treatments." A natural and logical next step. Instead, Abby and Rob made a decision that did not involve a newborn at all. They went right to the second part of their family plan. In Abby's words "we decided that we'd rather spend the money on raising a child or children who needed a home rather than spending it on the risky chance of maybe having a biological child of our own."

Abby and Rob knew they had the love, time, and commitment. They decided to pursue county adoption. Reason, "We knew these were kids that could use the good, loving home that we had to offer."

So, instead of a new baby, their first child was a five-year-old little girl. A girl from Wednesday's Child, Madison.

A Family Follow-up

Years later I got to see it all firsthand. I got to go home with the "Smiths." It was a rare opportunity for this reporter to follow-up on one of our adoptive families.

I'd met the children when they were in foster care. They were a profile segment on my television news story as we looked to find them a forever home. Later, we covered their in-court adoption day. Over the years, I saw this adoptive family at our annual Six Flags Magic Mountain reunion. By then, they were TV regulars and I'd air clips on their life story in compilation pieces on our families.

Today's shoot was different. We'd be doing an in-depth "Smith" family follow-up for our newscast six years after adoption. Madison had won a school essay contest, and we thought it would be a perfect look-back. An answer to the question "Does domestic adoption work? Does Wednesday's Child work?" Especially since her essay was her take on adoption, her own story. It was perfect for a WC success story.

Heading for Home

My engine was revving! Today was a big deal! Meeting up with Madison, seeing the "Smith" family victory was a highlight of my year.

We covered very few follow-ups, as that wasn't the job of Wednesday's Child. WC was a recruitment segment. As reporter/producer/host my job was limited to that. The WC goal was to profile a child in foster care who was looking for a forever home. My job was largely then done. Yet, it often left me wondering "whatever happened to so-and-so?"

It could take a year, even years, before a child may find a permanent place to call home. Some never do. Bottom line, back then, I rarely knew what the outcome was for the children we'd profiled. When we did learn of an adoption doing a follow-up news story was optional. However, the Freddie Mac Foundation contract did require us to cover a few per year.

Getting to see Madison years after adoption, at her home, was a luxury, and a joy!

My photographer and I jumped in our cars and made our way up north, a forty-five minute drive to the suburbs. I exited the freeway, passed modern strip malls, schools, and soccer fields. As I pulled up their street I sensed the neighborhood was just that, a neighborhood. With sidewalks for strolls, welcoming two-story middle class homes, and the occasional bike in the driveway, I smiled, my heart was content. I was happy for these children.

The "Smiths" eagerly greeted me at their front door.

Inside it was pleasant, as my eyes scanned the room. Family photos adorned the wall. Dogs in the backyard peered through the sliding glass door and whimpered for our attention. Games were stacked on shelves in the living room, kids toys taking over. The boys share a bedroom, and you'll find all kinds of boy toys. Madison has her own room and it's very girly. Homey and kid-friendly, I found it a safe place for the heart and soul. A safe place for a kid to just be a kid.

That's what domestic adoption is all about. Creating families. A forever place to call home, through thick and thin, but not without troubles. Kids growing up, maybe getting married, getting a job, having babies, parents becoming grandparents. Home for holidays. All the things that scream family! The kind you see on TV, the kind you read about, the kind kids dream about. It's the American dream. And it was years in the making.

Wednesday's Child

Let me take you back to our original shoot. I'd be showcasing the three siblings in foster care, ages four, three, and one. The children lived in different foster homes, and seeing each other this way was more of a forced interaction versus a natural brother and sister relationship where you know each other inside and out. There was a bit of chaos. First off, seeing one another probably provided extra energy, perhaps anxiety. I'd arrived late so I'm sure they were antsy. As I recall, they were a bit unruly and became overwhelming for me.

Will, was by now the long-time WC coordinator, and remembers it with a chuckle and ribs me about it constantly. He insists I left that day in frustration, threw my hands up in the air, walked away after the shoot and said with utter despair, "They're yours!"

We had gone to the Aquarium of the Pacific in Long Beach. It is a fabulous gem for Southern California where one can enjoy the beauty of sea life. For this bunch it might have been a bit too much. First off, they might have been a tad too young. Will says that Joey, only a year-and-a-half old, tried to jump in the shark tank petting pool; Will caught him in mid-air by the t-shirt. I vaguely recall the children running all over the place and being barely able to sit them still for a quickie interview.

I cringe at admitting this, but I believe I left wondering who'd be willing to adopt such a chaotic bunch?

In defense of the children I believe I had kept them waiting a bit. Not an easy thing for toddlers with their tiny attention span. Add that to the fact that there is a lot of walking and it was a long drive for the kids just to get there.

Plus, the Aquarium is a wonderful place to see and be, but a little bit harder to shoot a TV segment calling for interaction. There are few creatures tiny kids can touch. Unlike a pony ride, you can't ride a dolphin. A petting zoo here means petting starfish and rays. Fish are beautiful to the eye, but not exactly cuddly.

To say they had little interest in sitting still for a TV interview with some strange lady is an understatement. They wanted to run off and see the sea lions. Could you blame them!?

I returned to work and put the story together for on-air. That required boiling down the video and editing the short interview in a minute-thirty piece for the Wednesday's Child segment.

The Right Kids

Abby and Rob were viewers of Fox 11 News, and knowing they wanted to adopt they tuned in every week to see the WC segment. By that time, it had aired for over ten years with hundreds and hundreds of children being profiled.

Abby's take on my chaotic little bunch was in complete contrast to my own encounter. To my surprise where I saw headache she saw exactly what she was looking for. Abby says, "The sparkle in the eyes of that little girl looking at the fish with her brothers just called to us."

That is the beauty of Wednesday's Child. That is an example of what keeps me going. So often the children I see as most challenging are the exact ones someone else sees as a son or daughter.

The examples are heartwarming. There is one story of a sweet little boy with severe medical issues and a short life-span. He was adopted by a woman who didn't want him to die without knowing a mother's love. Another mom, Ann Belles, adopted two teenage boys, sixteen and seventeen, both severely autistic. Getting any teenage boy adopted is a challenge, let alone severely autistic ones. They were adopted just days before the eldest was to emancipate and be out on the streets. Now, they had somewhere to call home, and more important, someone to love. In fact, she's adopted a total of fifty kids, all with special needs. That is a whole book within itself!

I thank God I'm not in this alone. I thank God for people like Abby and Rob, for all the people who have adopted, whether from WC or any other foster child recruitment program. They see beauty and hope in our children, they see future and family. They see a need and answer the call.

They initially intended to adopt one child but when the "Smiths" watched WC that evening from their home they said, "Yes!" We want all three. All three!

A Match

Having already done all of the necessary background checks they'd already met county approval. That in itself is a lengthy process with background checks, home safety inspections, and references needed. Rob calls it "a bit stressful at times for us. It's never easy having a stranger decide if your home is good enough for these kids, or if you're good enough to be their parents."

The next step is what we call "a match." Were both sides a good fit? After meetings with their social worker and the in-depth info on the children, the answer was yes. They were a good "match." Abby and Rob were willing to put in the work. They were willing to funnel the energy, work on the wounds, teach the lessons, build the bonds, and to enforce the rules. To set the boundaries, open their home, offer a hug, wipe away a tear, provide shelter and safety... to be a mom and a dad and to love unconditionally.

But to do so also meant they had to buy a bigger house in order to adopt all three. You don't have to be rich to adopt, but you do need to provide a safe place to call home. There are restrictions on how many bedrooms are needed per child. Certainly, the little girl would need a separate room from the boys.

Abby describes the process as slow... then suddenly, very fast. The segment aired in September. They had meetings with social workers in October and November and then in December it was on!

"We got a call from our social worker saying there was an urgent need to get our daughter out of the foster care home she was in. Two days later, day one, we visited her at her foster home. Day two we visited again and brought her home with us for an overnight stay. Day three we went and got her things and she's been with us ever since."

With the boys, it was almost as fast. "A month after our daughter moved in, the county decided they wanted to move pretty quickly on the boys as well. Again, day one we went for a visit." At two years old, poor little Joey thought they were stealing him. Even so, "Joey spent our entire first visit wanting me to hold him," recalls Abby. Austin's take when they met, "Who are you?" Abby continues, "Day two we came to visit again and brought them home for an overnight visit. Day three we took them back to their foster home. Day four we went to get them and their things and they came to live with us."

"We went from zero to three children in five weeks."

You see now why I call the "Smiths" an "instant family?"

Wow! That's a shocking change to life, for everyone! Says Abby, "at first it was… yikes! Not only did we suddenly have a house full of kids, but they hadn't seen each other in six months since their Wednesday's Child segment was filmed."

Since the children lived in different foster homes that meant they had to get reacquainted each time they got together. No brother and sister should have to go through that, yet it's often a reality in the case of foster care. Everything possible is done to keep siblings together, but sometimes it just doesn't happen.

Abby describes their initial group get-togethers like this. "The few times the kids did see each other, they spent the time playing in their own little world where to them the outside world didn't exist. Then, they were separated and taken to their foster homes. It was very hard at first to get them to understand and realize that they were now living together and learn to interact with the outside world even though they were together."

The Reality of County Adoption

Adoption for the "Smith" family came when the children were six, five, and three.

Perhaps now is a good time to explain why I've been writing their family name with quotation marks. "Smith" is not their real last name. It is a protective name. We call them the "Smith" family to protect them from the past. To allow them all to move forward in peace.

> "We get to celebrate and share in these young people's lives thanks to this segment highlight on a weekly basis."
>
> Nicole, WC viewer

When all parties met there was still contact with the birth mother. There were supervised visits allowed by the courts. Abby indicates it didn't go well. "It got to the point that none of the kids even wanted to go for the visits." When parental rights were terminated the adoption proceeded, but slowly. Says Rob, "With the boys having been in one foster home and our daughter in another, that meant two sets of paperwork, two social workers, two CASA's (volunteer advocates on behalf of the children), and it took quite a while for all the i's to get dotted and the t's to get crossed and all the paperwork straightened out. We finally had to push a little bit so we could get the adoption finalized before the school year started. The judge who had been handling the case was great. She took it upon herself to make sure the kids were adopted before they went back to school after summer break. She worked us in on a special day with her regular cases, not waiting for the regular adoption day."

The story of foster care is often one of turmoil, troubles, courts, police, protective custody, visitation, severance, social workers, foster families, new people... and I'm sure much sadness. In simple terms, children in foster care come from birth families that were unable to care for them. That is deemed by the courts.

So back to the "Smith" children. They are an example of a story just right for Wednesday's Child. Three siblings. Three toddlers. Such a scenario would be considered "hard to place." You're asking someone to take on an instant family. No breaking in period of a newborn.

I love this perspective from Darnell's dad. "The beauty of older children, no diapers!"

We Are Family

When do you start feeling like you are family? I've found each family's answer to that question to be different. For Abby and Rob "we realized it the second we met them and took them home. The minute they walked in the door… they were family. For *them* to realize that this was home, that took some time."

For the parents, adoption has been months or years in the making, a joyous occasion. For the children, this can be the latest in a strange new home with strange new adults. Joey was a toddler and remembers being greeted by the big dogs when he arrived at his new home. He recalls that he felt "scared because I thought that the dogs were going to bite us." Madison also remembers the dogs. "I was scared because all the dogs were barking, but after a couple of days I was used to it" she says. The fact they'd been in numerous foster homes already, and had experienced trauma in being separated from their birth family, added to the stress they were already under. On many occasions, foster children I've interviewed still express love for their birth mom and dad. Some still have a loyalty... despite the abuse, abandonment or neglect. It's a fact, most children love their mommies and daddies and may not even understand why they can't be in their birth home. Madison seems to have a good understanding of it all. As to why she was in foster care, she says, "My birth mom didn't take good care of me."

Abby and Rob got a mixed bag. Their youngest had not been in many foster homes. "Joey was two when we took him home so he doesn't remember much," says Mom. Not the same story for the older two. Abby says "it took some time before the older two fully felt like they weren't going anywhere. Even after the adoption was finalized the two older ones still worried that someone was going to come and take them away." While that may have been a lingering fear, Austin also tells me he had the feeling when he first moved in that he was "home at last." He was happy.

Still they were ironing out the bugs. Austin says he was convinced this was home "after the adoption." Madison's memory was "The minute I stepped into my new house I knew it was home." Keep in mind, she answered this question six years after being adopted. Sounds to me like Abby and Rob have built a place of comfort, confidence and consistency. But Abby says for the "Smith" family to feel like family it actually took two to three years.

Parenting

An instant family means there is no growing together at first like you'd have with a newborn. Instead, you come with your values and rules, and the children come with theirs. Abby knows that firsthand. "The one thing I can tell you is they will test you and their teachers. They have to see just how much they can get away with." Abby's advice is "As long as you stand firm, show them who's in charge and don't let them get away with anything, they will stop pretty fast. You can't make a child respect you, you have to earn their respect. I've seen other parents who 'babied' the kids they adopted and now a few years later the kids are so out of control and have no respect for anyone, including their adoptive parents."

Add another layer to that. Since the children were in separate foster homes each was different in their approach. Abby cites this example: "one of my kids liked the negative attention, the bigger the drama the better. We realized that all we or the teacher had to do was quietly give out the consequence without anyone else knowing, and after handling the situation like this a couple of times, the behavior all but disappeared." She adds that "The boys came to us having no discipline, no rules and no respect for female authority. Our home became a mini boot camp. It took a good three months before the boys began to learn some rules and respect. (It helped after we got the abscessed tooth removed from our older son, and had the rocks, gum and gum wrappers removed from his ears so he could hear better.) Our daughter came from a home where she had to lie to survive. She was so good at it that you knew she was lying; you just couldn't catch her at it. But, we learned that if you let her think you believe her even when you know she is lying, she'll relax and slip up. Once we began catching her every time, she got tired of lying and pretty much quit."

For the children it is an adjustment too. Everything was new.

The hardest part about the adjustment period for Austin, the middle boy, was all "the rules." He was four when they met. He's now ten and understands better what he went through. I asked the little one to tell me what the hardest part was for him. Joey said "getting used to them holding me." Mom remembers it differently. "Joey spent his first year always asking to be held." For Madison, the hardest part was "getting to know my new Mom and Dad."

I was thinking as an adult how hard it is to move, to meet new neighbors, forge new friendships and feel comfortable in a strange environment. Imagine being a child and doing it several times, with new "parents," often times under stressful conditions.

Boundaries Are Essential

Not being a parent myself, when it comes to rules and parenting, I have to take Abby and Rob's word for it. One look at their children and you know they are doing something right. Ask the children their take.

Madison got the message, she says she learned "not to lie, behave yourself and love who you are." Joey will tell you he's learning "what not to do and what to do." Austin learned these concepts, "Don't be rude, be nice to other people, always have good manners and try your best."

Rob has this great reminder, "there are days where you think you are the worst parent in the world, especially those first few months when you're ignored unless you're yelling. But, it gets better and you begin to have some days where you think you have this parenting thing down pretty good. But, don't be fooled, you'll still have those 'bad' parenting days every once in a while. Most of the days are going to be somewhere in the middle."

Like every parent, you want your child to be happy. Seeing that joy is one of Abby's greatest pleasures. "They are mostly laughing, joking, teasing or smiling with us and each other. They are (now) so relaxed, at peace and comfortable. The kids rarely fight… but they do tattle and bicker with each other."

Sounds like children, just being children. That's the ultimate goal of adoption!

Years Later

The "Smith" family has settled in quite nicely. Thanks to our reunions I continue to get yearly updates. I get to witness this family growing up.

My image is always of Mom Abby bouncing up in comfortable clothes with her warm and energetic smile. The kids quietly tag along for another date at one of LA's great theme parks or activities. Dad is always there. And always Uncle Jeff, Abby's brother, too. Both Abby and Rob are great interviews and willing to give us a family review. The kids too are kind enough to give a quick chat on camera. I soak in the updates that tell me all is well.

Says Abby, "our daughter enjoys dancing, and has even tried teaching a few steps to her brothers, which is quite entertaining to watch. Our oldest son is now a junior black belt in Tae Kwon Do. He will be a black belt before he's twelve years old. I have a stack of broken boards from all of his tests. His last few tests, we have just seen a huge increase in his confidence level that has also transferred, somewhat, into his schoolwork. It was really impressive seeing him break a board with a kick and send pieces of it flying, and then breaking one with his elbow, which he had never tried to do before, on the first attempt. Our youngest son is also in Tae Kwon Do and is currently a brown belt, only four away from his black belt."

If he stays with it, the oldest boy, Austin, will have learned long-term life lessons. He says he wants to be "a Tae Kwon Do Master." Little Joey would like to be a firefighter when he grows up. Madison wants to be, "a lot of things, like a dancer, dolphin trainer and a model for things. Oh, and an actor."

I often thought about this family and what made them special, and then one day it hit me! The children were different now. Not the same children from our initial meeting, from our Wednesday's Child shoot. They were confident, secure, well behaved, healthy, interesting and growing. They were just children. They had a mom and a dad, went to school, were involved in activities, had relatives. This was a normal family... if there is such a thing, and an instant one, at that.

An Award Winner

As part of a school assignment, Madison wrote an essay about her family. It earned her a district wide award, a beautiful blue ribbon and a ton of confidence. You can read her essay in the chapter titled, "From the Heart of a Child."

The honor was the reason for my family visit, the reason for my next news report, and for this rare family follow-up. It gave this hardened reporter hope for all children in foster care. It showed me the power of a good adoption. It was proof Wednesday's Child was working. I returned to the news station to write my story... and coined this family that came together so quickly, "The Instant Family."

> "It's priceless to see them grow up with aspirations and goals to finish school and have a family one day."
>
> Angel, WC viewer

The Often Family

"The Instant Family" can now also be called "The Often Family" as I tend to see them often, at least at our every event. Abby says they wouldn't miss an event because, after all, "it's family!" She means the Wednesday's Child family. As I continued my soul-searching, Abby and I had a recent talk about "the tough times." I asked a difficult question, "You don't have to answer as if this were you, but does anyone ever wish they hadn't adopted?" Of course I was thinking of my own family's tough times.

"NOOOOooooo," she said long and drawn out. "I can't imagine where my children would be without me!" she said incredulously.

I pondered the thought for days before calling my mother. I posed the very same concept. Despite all the pain and heartache his lifestyle had caused, her philosophy on my brother was, "perhaps he did the best he could. He might have been worse off." I asked why she ran to him on his last day. "Because I cared about him." As for legal family "we were all he had."

Knowing my concern Abby later wrote me a wonderful note. "We knew it wasn't going to be easy 100 percent of the time when we adopted these kids, but they needed us as much as we needed them. And we'll get through each challenge. No matter how it turns out, we'll know we did our best and that's what counts."

Thanks Abby for the life lesson. Thanks to my adoptive parents for helping me understand my own parents.

Melissa and Crystal on adoption day

Chapter 14

Our American Girl Family—The Newtons

"Patty-cake, patty-cake, bakers man." Our hands slapped together as we sang the old English nursery rhyme.

"Bake me a cake as fast as you can." At five years old, Melissa knew those words well. Her tiny hands clapped against mine. Her soft childlike voice rang soft and sweet.

"Roll the dough and mark it with B, and throw it in the oven for baby and me."

It was during her Wednesday's Child profile interview that we played Patty cake. It was also her "Dream Day". Location... a doll store. Not just any doll store, American Girl Place. If you've never been, let me paint the picture. American Girl Place is heaven on earth if you love dolls. It's two-stories tall, with a corner mall location at The Grove in Los Angeles. A dressed-up doll can run over $100. There's a doll for every interest. The cowgirl, the cheerleader, the hula dancer, the surfer. We were like "kids in a candy store."

To my surprise this little girl looked every bit the little doll herself. She was wearing powder pink. The dress. The soft sweater. Her hair had been styled to perfection. Puffy pony tails on each side of her head. Pink ribbons sticking out. A ringlet hung down the right side of her face. I'm guessing her foster mom got her "all dolled up."

I leaned over with my lanky 5'9" frame and sweetly asked "Do you know which doll you want?"

"Yes," she said confidently.

"What does she look like?" I asked.

Melissa answered, "she looks just like me."

Melissa picked out her perfect doll. The beauty of American Girl Place is that there is wonderful variety. Long hair, short hair, pony tail, braids, blond, brunette, redhead, curly haired, straight, kinky haired. The dolls came in every skin tone too. Melissa selected the doll with this description: Dark skin, curly dark brown hair, brown eyes. She was right, it did indeed look just like her.

Next, we dressed our doll. Melissa selected a "Special Occasion" dress. It was elegant. Cream colored with a satin sash, a full skirt with tulle underneath. Ballet-flat shoes. She'd picked a dress fit for a princess because, "she looks pretty." Melissa named her doll, Emily.

I'll never forget Melissa's "Dream Day". It was picture perfect in every way. A Hollywood ad agency couldn't have scripted it better. Viewers loved it and loved her. We got more calls on Melissa than perhaps any other child ever profiled. She was beyond adorable!

My hope was that Melissa's story would speak volumes for the hundreds of other children in foster care. The children not on the news. The children also waiting for someone to call. My hope was that Melissa would find the right match. On Wednesday's Child, we do everything in our power to convey the personality of our unique kids. Will Wong says it best when he describes what we do.

> We tailor the WC shoots specific to the child's interests so we can bring out their best, to help the public connect with them. It's a very human thing to gravitate towards someone who has similar interests, and to promote a child within the realm of their interests can help them connect with a family that will best meet their needs. Everyone already assumes the

> bad stuff associated with our kids, and for the most part those assumptions are somewhat true, given their history of abuse and neglect. However, much of it is also "imagined" or erroneously assumed by the public, so this is an opportunity for our kids to shine in their elements, in the realm of what they are interested in to make that first connection.
>
> My role is to make the process therapeutic for the child and to ensure that the child feels good about the process going in and coming out of it. When it came to Melissa's shoot, there was no doubt we'd captured the essence of the little girl she was.

It wasn't until two years later, that I got a call with happy news. Melissa was getting adopted! Will announced it would happen on National Adoption Day. I was thrilled to know her journey through the system had come to an end, thrilled to know she had found a forever family.

Family for Melissa meant a mom, Crystal Newton. Crystal is a single parent, reflecting L.A. County's progressive policy of allowing people who are unmarried to adopt. Crystal is a dedicated, kind and loving mother. She has worked wonders in bringing out Melissa's inner beauty to match her outer. "It wasn't always easy," said Crystal.

> My faith in God has been with me since the beginning. I asked God for a house where I could raise my children. Didn't know if I could afford it or maintain a house and child. But He supplied me with the house and I kept my word by following through with adopting. He's been taking care of us ever since. My favorite song is 'Blessed Assurance Jesus Is Mine' an oldie but a goodie, as they say. For me, it's a heartfelt song as I would always sing it in my head when I got

> worried about the adoption process. If God was with me, I knew I could make it through.

On her adoption day, National Adoption Day, Melissa and Mom arrived hand-in-hand. To my delight, Melissa was again "all dolled up." She wore a light colored tea-length dress and powder-pink sweater. So did her doll. Yes indeed, after two years, Melissa still had Emily, her American Girl doll. This time doll and daughter were dressed exactly the same.

> Adopting a child in the system was not an easy process for me. My journey has shown me that if I could reach this goal, any other goals can be reached and will be worth it as well. It takes persistence, commitment, patience and perseverance. Adoption day was unbelievable, exciting and well worth waiting for. There were so many children being adopted on National Adoption Day, I know Melissa felt like a shining star in a galaxy. For me, it was like I found the pot of gold at the end my journey… my Melissa.

I asked Crystal why she wanted to adopt in the first place.

> I had many friends as a child in elementary school, but one classmate, a little girl, will always stay in my mind forever. We were friends for a very short period of time. She came to my classroom as a new student in the middle of the school year, and as soon as we were building our friendship, within a month or so, she was gone. While I really don't know if she was in the foster care system, I remember she was different. Now looking back she had the signs of a foster child; not very talkative, didn't want to play as much and seemed sad and lonely. I wanted to have

her as my friend because I wanted her to fit in and become happy.

Another experience was with a close friend of my mother's that was a 'single' foster parent. When we went over to her house, her (foster) children seemed happy and I wanted to be with them because they were around my age and seemed to be having fun all the time. Even though they were of different nationalities she treated them as though they were her own. She had one daughter and fostered both boys and girls.

Both of these experiences somehow have influenced me to help children in need of a stable home environment. Why shouldn't they have a secure and happy childhood?

How did you come upon Melissa? Why?

After completing my state and county requirements, and attending the required courses, I found myself waiting for a call from my first assigned social worker. I attended all the Adoption Fairs I could, enlisted the help of my friends and co-workers, listened to the radio and watched TV announcements. I waited for a year and nothing happened. Eventually, I requested a change in social worker. While waiting for my new social worker, I had inquired about a young teenager. (Not what I had requested in my profile, but I was willing to take a chance.) A short experience with the teenager did not last long, eight months to be exact. It made me rethink about adopting since I was now in my second year of what seemed like a dead-end.

When I got the call from Fenella, my new social worker, I expressed my expectations. We communicated well. She was on point. She called me within a few weeks and told me about Melissa. The long wait was now what I was seeing, on a small photo. This beautiful little girl had the prettiest smile and sandy brown hair, just like mine when I was a child. So I called and wanted to meet Melissa as soon as I was able. Every weekend that I could pick her up from her foster home and take her to my house, I did.

Was there an adjusting period?

Actually we're still in an adjusting period. It's been two years and there's always some situation that comes up and our discussions can be lengthy. I take it with a grain of salt, pepper, sugar, and allspice. (LOL) She is in transition therapy once a week with T.I.E.S for Adoption and it has helped us a lot. It's important to know that there are going to be issues to address and adoptive parents don't need to go it alone.

For example, after a year of adoption placement and several months after our official adoption date, Melissa still struggles with her 'separation' issues (from her birth mother/family). She has crying spells, longing for her birth mother, missing her brothers. At times she has problems sleeping in her own bed and in the room by herself. Having to deal with these and other types of issues are difficult, and I never expected the hurt and sorrow to last this long. I stress the fact that I love her, that her additional family loves her and we want the best for her.

My immediate goal for Melissa is that she realizes she is my daughter, I am her mom and I love her unconditionally. That she knows God loves her. That she is in a nurturing, stable, secure and trustworthy home, and that I will do whatever it takes for her to have the best education, and that nothing can stop her from reaching her goals. She knows that I expect her to do her best in life and to give back in community service by volunteering in areas where she sees a need. She needs to know I expect her to give respect and learn to teach others to respect her, too. As a child she carries a lot of self- blaming and she can only use her situation to encourage others to overcome their fear of separation and self-blame.

It was not easy but I noticed overtime (years) the bad dreams, insecurities, 'out of the blue' crying for birth family members, slowly was replaced by good dreams, funny dreams, self-esteem, and self-confidence kicked in. I thank God, her previous foster mother, her brothers closest to her and their grandfather who took her in even though they are not biologically related. They kept up positive attitudes with her. I promised her I would continue to let her see and talk to her brothers and I have.

What are your dreams for your daughter?

My dream for Melissa is that she understands and can deal with life's ups and downs maturely and logically. That she can trust and depend on God as her Heavenly Father, and that she can trust and depend on me as her mother.

I wouldn't trade this experience for anything. And who knows, I just might adopt again :).

Our Dream Dolls

Melissa's adoption was my last to cover before writing this book. As I enter my sixteenth year of adoption reporting, I think it's safe to say she is not the last.

Oh, and by the way, as Melissa has her doll, I now have one too! Will saw the fascination in my eyes on that "Dream Day" shoot. For my birthday he gave me my very own American Girl doll. And yes, it was dressed like me, looked like me. Will chose a career gal outfit and knows I will one day go buy it a frilly girl dress or pretty princess dress just like Melissa did.

The doll sits on my dresser where I see it each and every day. It has been a long time since I've had a doll. As usual Will knows how to bring out the Chrissy in me, the little girl who grew up to be this unlikely adoption advocate, this cheerleader for children. GO TEAM WC!

Epilogue

Finding a Forever Family

TEAM WC is a team constantly at practice and in search of new members. The game we play affects real lives, and while it can be a rough sport there are so many sweet victories worthy of celebration. So, as I end this book let's pop the champagne and cheer on all the nation's families who've ever adopted children from foster care. Let's hoist the children high above the elated fans and honor their existence. Let's rally our teammates in this journey we call real life.

I once had a journalism teacher in high school who lectured me "Christine, there's more to life than cheerleading." On this day, and in this way, I couldn't disagree more. If we aren't cheering on our nation's children, who is? Finding a Forever Family is by no means The Superbowl, the game at the end of the season. It is more the sport, the game of life, with a rich and long history and a season ahead.

Already, we have our next adoption in the works. Will got word that a little boy we'd profiled was just placed into the home of his potential parents-to-be. I remembered the boy well from his "Dream Day", and he was a reminder we still had work to do. We were on the field at the L.A. Dodgers batting practice. The little guy was so quiet, yet present. His large eyes took it all in, but he would only allow a stiff half-smile, no matter how much we prodded. As I was about to leave him and head back to work this child suddenly spoke up. Surprised, I stopped in my tracks.

I turned and looked down at his precious little face, and my five-foot-nine inch frame leaned over as he craned his little neck to look up at me, squinted his eyes, and inquired ever so innocently:

"When am I gonna see you again?"

Once again my heart melted as it continues to do on a regular basis (and yes, he looked a lot like Mike). I'm excited at the idea he now is inches away from a forever family. YEA TEAM WC! Another win on-the-way for the record books!

Not only was I an unlikely adoption advocate, it was highly unlikely I'd ever put pen to paper. "You should write a book," said my attorney, Emily Card. I scrunched up my face with a look of disdain. "Write a book? I'm not sure I have anything to say. Who would read it and who cares?" Emily and I had this discussion often over the years and often I was convinced I had no story to tell. When she'd asked me to envision my epitaph I knew it would include something of service, after all, it was the family way. As I watch my family members I see how each has "made a difference" in their very own way. Grandpa gave his garden vegetables away for free. Danielle is a wonderful mother. Dad insisted on education. Skylar gives me little-kid colorings. Lance is a leader, and the man of the family. Grandma kept a beautiful country home. Mom is wise with words I hear nowhere else. B.T. is my side-kick. Sean continues to fulfill his promise that "life will never be dull." All are proof we make a difference in the lives we encounter.

If I should be so lucky as to leave a legacy it would be this. I envision my work on-air inspiring at least one person to want to give back. You don't have to adopt to make a difference. One can mentor, one can volunteer, one can simply do their job well, or even offer up a kind and unexpected gesture. I once knew a celebrity who did zero community service, but still gave back in a welcomed way. He arrived to work every day with a smile for all, a joke to tell, and a laugh that was infectious. To me, that was a tremendous gift that I got to unwrap each and every day. Giving back can be as easy as that.

"For such a time as this." I never envisioned God might be placing me in Los Angeles for all the right reasons. While I hadn't pursued the big city I ended up here by walking through doors that seemed to open seamlessly. My dream was to be the home-town gal on the news back in Phoenix, but that never came to fruition. In fact, early on, I was told I was too green. And I was. And that is why I worked all that much harder when I hit Los Angeles. I sensed it was a gift of some sort but had no idea it would take me back to the world of adoption and foster care.

I'm a changed woman thanks to all the good people of Wednesday's Child, The Thomas', The Cates', The Diaz', The Smiths, The Newtons, The Freddie Mac Foundation, DCFS and all of the families, children, and "Dream Day" sponsors not mentioned who so inspired this book. Through TEAM WC I'm able to proudly answer an often heard complaint. "The news is so negative. There's nothing good in the news." I smile brightly and tell them to watch Wednesday's Child.

While Jared was our first adoption ambassador, the concept continues to live on large and strong. He will forever remain the wind-beneath-our wings. While Jared may be gone so many of the other children continue to light the fire of passion I have for the work we are doing. Take Darnell. This boy continues to wow by his every day actions; however, I must share two examples of how this boy is living the legacy. First example came at Christmas. For a second year in a row, he and his family got up early and went to see the homeless. That was before opening any presents. Let me paint the picture. I'm not talking about going to the safety of a shelter. I'm talking about the mean streets. The Cates drove downtown and found homeless men and women on the street just blocks away from L.A.'s very sorrowful Skid Row. Darnell had the idea to hand out Christmas cards. He'd personally signed all thirty-five cards. Darnell can't forget one man and he tells me the story with the biggest of eyes still in wonder. "I handed him the card, and he started to cry. And then he brought out his Bible and started reading." Darnell returned home with his mom and siblings that Christmas morning. "I didn't even want to open my presents."

Imagine how my heart sings as I hear of such stories. As I wrapped up this book I got to see Darnell in action one more time. The second example involves a women's mentoring organization called HerShe. They mentor girls in foster care and their proof of performance is a cotillion type Cinderella Ball. Cotillion is an education in etiquette, manners and formal dance originating out of France in the 1700s. (I'd *always* wanted to be in cotillion!) For the formal dance, the girls need a partner. That's where Darnell came in. He and his boys volunteered to stand-up for these girls, to be their escorts. It was such a stunning picture! Darnell entered the room dressed in a black tux, crisp white shirt and stood ever so tall, she in an elegant white gown worthy of any wedding. Darnell was indeed a gentleman escorting a refined and lovely young lady as she was presented to society. I was one proud God-mama. At the end I rushed to give him a hug and take a picture. The other young men gathered 'round too. Darnell introduced me, not as Christine Devine on the news, but said, "This is my god-mom."

It's a funny thing to think about where we find "family." And the cotillion story brings me back to my past. In high school I was invited to join cotillion and was thrilled to be in such company. My mother with her farm girl roots was having none of it. Plus, she said "we couldn't afford it." As I told Mom all about Darnell's day she retorted with a chuckle. "See, you got to go to cotillion after all!"

To those considering adopting, I hope you now have a realistic picture of the puzzle and an understanding of the missing pieces. To those who have adopted, I hope you found a kinship with your fellow family members, for we are indeed all one. For those unsure of adopting, I hope you see that adoption itself brings uncertainty, but so does life. May we all go through the process of discovery with the love and support of someone who cares. To the children from foster care, I hope that you understand you teach each and every one of us, just by being.

In a perfect world, I'd work with children and families before they ever reached the system. I'd put myself out of business. And if I could turn back time for Mike I would do so. I'd mentioned he was a natural born artist. One year, having no money, he sketched my portrait for a present. It hangs on my wall as a reminder that he, too, had a gift. No child should enter earth the way he did. Yes, he was responsible for the choices he would go on to make, yet I can't help but hurt over what could have been. That hurt keeps me crusading for these kids.

I marvel at how we all walk our own walk. It is no secret in my family that my mom never wanted me to work in television. She'd so wanted me to be a rocket scientist. We joke about it to this day. Not gonna happen! I do hope, however, that I am fulfilling one of Mom's mantras. "To whom much is given, much is expected." Having lived in Brazil's favelas, she made sure that we knew we had much. As I wrote this book, Mom and I had many a discussion and I'm moved by the tremendous and unexpected amount of healing that occurred in our relationship. I came to the great conclusion that I no longer see myself as that little girl wanting and failing to please Mommy. While science still will never be my thing, writing is. Early on, I'd thought perhaps I'd be like Mom and Dad and teach. Then I'd thought about news. It is like constantly being in class, a kind of school of current events. I am humbled and honored to have been chosen to write the stories of Wednesday's Child. Mom perhaps paid me the greatest of compliments recently when she said, "Thanks for insisting on being you."

I'm hoping for more books to come. Perhaps I'll write *The Foster Care Chronicles* next. I've also realized I could write an entire book just on Jared. There isn't a week that goes by that I don't remember this kid. Our photo is framed in my TV room. The family flag from his funeral is folded neatly into a flag box and sits on my shelf. With him in mind, my last Wednesday's

Child shoot before submitting this book was on a little boy who looked surprisingly like Jared and was about the same age. He had the same thin little arms, milky white skin, and spiked short hair. Would you believe, just like Jared's shoot, this one was at a hockey game. This kid got his own jersey. This boy went VIP on the ice. As the memory of Jared hit me fast and hard I flashed an incredulous look at Will as if to say, *you're kidding me, right?* I thought *God must really be sending me a message to never forget the mission!*

Then, this beautiful little boy with the biggest green eyes, the longest of lashes, a freckled face and a sweet little-kid voice asked a question. "Is this my special day?"

"Yes sweetie, it is." And I knew once again a child's life had been changed forever.

Study Guide

I hope you've enjoyed reading *Finding A Forever Family* either alone, with your family or Reading Group. I've included this *Study Guide* section to help you apply this book to your personal lives. Get cozy, grab a journal, get together with friends and share your answers. I hope these questions inspire further thought and stir up an invigorating discussion.

Christine Devine

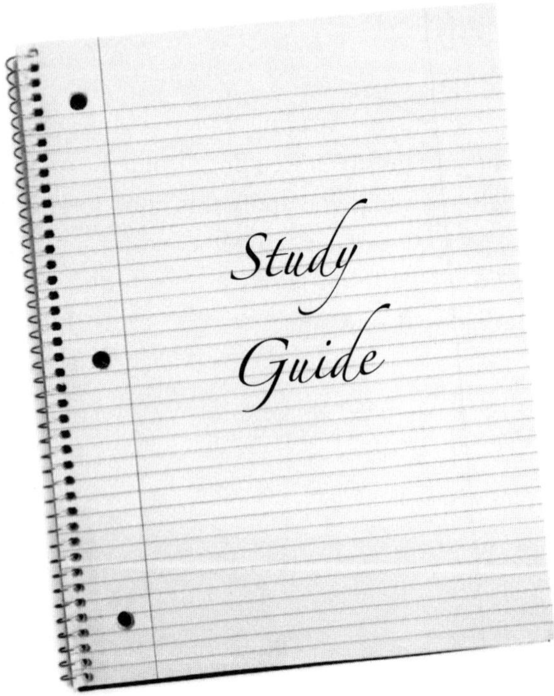
Study
Guide

INTRODUCTION

1. Like Christine, can you think back to a time you were asked to do a job you didn't really want to do? How did you respond?

2. Are you a yes man... woman? Are you a people pleaser?

3. Christine loves her news director. Who was your favorite boss?

4. Does your work become personal?

5. Christine thought adoption meant "a happy ending." How do you view adoption?

CHAPTER ONE – WEDNESDAY'S CHILD

1. How do you view the nightly news?

2. Are there elements of the positive in your city's newscast?

3. Like Christine, do you have a family secret or relative who's caused pain or trauma?

4. How do you separate professional and personal?

5. Christine was asked the question "What would your epitaph read?" What would YOURS say?

CHAPTER TWO – HOW IT ALL BEGINS

1. We saw how The Freddie Mac Foundation is of service. How are you giving back to your community?

2. Where does the support come for your efforts?

3. Like a child in foster care, imagine what it must be like to be away from your birth family.

4. Imagine turning eighteen and being out in the world with no family. How would you cope?

5. Have you known any social workers or children in foster care?

CHAPTER THREE – THE CHILDREN OF FOSTER CARE

1. How do feel when you read of a parent abusing a child?

2. This chapter talks of children still longing for their birth parent, even an abusive parent. Can you describe a child's love for Mommy and Daddy?

3. Life can be hard. Discuss some of life's challenges.

4. Christine had an "Esther conclusion." Did you ever have a time where you discovered you were exactly where you were supposed to be?

5. Christine sought answers to her questions. Where do you turn for understanding?

CHAPTER FOUR – WATCHDOG WILL

1. Do you have a Batman to your Robin? A partner "on-the-job?"

2. Will Wong shares his success with his colleagues. With whom do you share your success?

3. Did you ever have a friendship that was slow to develop?

4. Christine gave Will a tough time. Was there ever anyone in life you should have been nicer to?

5. Whom do you turn to with all of your secrets?

CHAPTER FIVE – MEETING JARED

1. Christmas in this chapter meant a news segment. Describe your Christmas.

2. Name a cool, courageous kid you know.

3. For the Thomas' Jared was their Christmas gift. Describe a memorable Christmas gift.

4. Jared was inspired to take up hockey. Was there something in your life that inspired you in a certain direction?

5. We read of Jared growing up. Describe your kids, or nieces/nephews, or siblings, growing up.

CHAPTER SIX – A WEDNESDAY'S CHILD GROWS UP

1. Jared entered Christine's life on a personal level. Describe an unexpected friendship in your life.

2. What do you hope to inspire in your kids, or colleagues?

3. Jared was thrilled to meet Tommy Lasorda of the Dodgers. Who would you like to meet?

4. Have you read *A Purpose Driven Life*? If so, what did you get out of it?

5. Was there a moment where you felt you were really living life to the fullest?

CHAPTER SEVEN – LOSING JARED

1. Little Rock was home to Maureen. Is there a place you've always considered "home?"

2. Has there ever been a tragedy in your life?

   If yes, how did you feel about the suddenness of it all?

3. How do you feel about teenagers behind the wheel?

4. Why is it we feel a young person who dies has been robbed of life?

5. Where would/do you turn in times of trouble?

CHAPTER EIGHT – REMEMBERING JARED

1. Are we moved differently when someone dies young?

2. How were you touched by the passing of someone special?

3. Has someone touched your life to the point they inspired you to live life in a fuller way?

4. We've all felt lucky or blessed to have a certain person in our lives. Who is that person?

5. How would you like to be remembered?

CHAPTER 9 – THE DEVINE FAMILY

1. "Mom" started documenting her life. Have you or your parents started your own personal memoir? What would it say?

2. Who's your favorite movie star and why?

3. Describe where you were born.

4. Talk about the memories of your grandparents or childhood.

5. Who in your family has had a profound influence on you and how?

CHAPTER 10 – MY L.A. FAMILY

1. What tells you your children are growing up?

2. Did you celebrate your sixteenth birthday?

3. Describe a party you've thrown at your home.

4. Do you have a big family or small?

5. Describe a favorite time at the dinner table.

CHAPTER 11 – MY DREAM FAMILY

1. Mary and Arthur both wanted to adopt. Share one thing you had in common with your spouse early on.

2. Darnell was asked, "What would you do with a million dollars?" What would YOU do?

3. Do you remember moving to a new school, new neighborhood?

4. Both Christine and Darnell learned some life lessons early on. Do you remember a childhood lesson?

5. Describe your happy home.

CHAPTER 12 – OUR FIRST FOUNDATION FAMILY

1. Did you/do you want lots of children?

2. Share some of the struggles of raising children.

3. What kinds of problems did you cause your parents?

4. How do you keep your family together?

5. If you have children, what are your goals for your children? If not, for yourself?

CHAPTER 13 – THE INSTANT FAMILY

1. If you couldn't have children would you consider fertility treatments?

2. What makes a home a place of comfort?

3. When are your children unruly?

4. How do you set boundaries in your relationships?

5. Describe activities you enjoyed as a child.

CHAPTER 14 – OUR AMERICAN GIRL

1. Do you recall a favorite nursery rhyme or children's story?

2. Did you have a favorite doll?

3. Crystal prayed for a home to raise her children. What do you currently pray for?

4. Melissa does a bit of self-blaming. Where do you see yourself do that?

5. Describe a meaningful gift someone gave you that you have to this day.

EPILOGUE

1. Are you thinking of adopting? Have you already adopted? Discuss the reasons why you took this route in life.

2. How did/would adoption change your family and/or your home?

3. Where would/do you turn in times of trouble?

4. Share the joys of parenting an adopted child. (For example, with adoption you have some unique firsts, such as the first time a child calls you "Mommy.")

5. If it truly takes a village, where would/do you turn for support and a parenting pick-me-up?

6. What was one "take away" or "Aha moment" you got from reading this book?

PART THREE

Appendices

WASHINGTON SALUTES CONGRESSIONAL COALITION HONOREES

From The White House:

"I am pleased to join you in honoring those who have opened their hearts to children in need. Families are the foundation upon which we build our lives. Giving a child a home, a family to love, and a safe place to grow is one of life's greatest and most generous gifts. As you celebrate this occasion and look towards the future, Michelle and I wish you all the best."

President Barack Obama

From The State Department:

"We need you Angels more than ever... We need you to help advise us on how to avoid the pitfalls that sometimes come from laws that are written but are not working in reality. We need your help in raising awareness about the kids in foster care and orphans in your own community."

Secretary of State Hillary Clinton

From U.S. Senate:

Christine Devine is a stalwart advocate for children in need. Her segment continues to help children find homes and draws attention to the critical issue of adoption. Her tireless work makes her truly worthy of this honor.

US Senator Dianne Feinstein, California- nominating Senator

National honorees include:
Laura Bush, Rosie O'Donnell, Hallmark Channel, Sesame Workshop, Sean & Lee Anne Touhy (The Blind Side story), and Al Roker (The Today Show); Christine Devine was an honoree from California.

Appendix A

Advice from Our Parents

The amazing parents featured in this book took time to answer a detailed questionnaire that I provided. Their heartfelt responses have been included throughout this book. It's safe to say that each of these WC parents is filled to the brim with helpful advice and guidance for others who might be traveling this journey. I suggest anyone wanting to adopt tap into the resources and support programs within their own communities. Until then, here are some things to think about.

I asked our parents what advice they would give to prospective parents, and what advice they have on navigating the system itself. Hopefully, prospective parents will walk away with some ideas on how to make a complex process go a little smoother.

Mary Cates

I would recommend that they keep an open mind, be patient with the adoption process, love your adoptive children as if they were your biological children, respect their opinions and make sure they understand what adoption means and why they had to be separated from their biological parents. Most of all, they need to know that it's okay to make mistakes, and that you love them no matter what happens.

The system doesn't always tell you about or how to tap into the numerous resources available to the family of adoptive children. Networking with other parents and researching opportunities online are incredibly valuable tools.

Richard Diaz

My advice would be expect the worst, appreciate everything else, and be totally committed. You have to be 100 percent committed to adoption or don't do it. I could write a small book on what "the system" didn't tell us about our kids, but what purpose would that serve? They left it up to us to find resources, so be prepared to do your own legwork, don't expect to get a detailed blueprint that outlines your kids' life. Even if they've been in the system for years, sometimes even the system doesn't know what's really going on in the mind and heart of your kid. Would we do it again, yes, and we have, and we will do it again given the opportunity.

Crystal Newton

I realized quickly that being consistent no matter what is critical. Bend the rules very little. Be prepared to explain. Remember, you'll have to break things down to their level. No's and stop's did not work for her, I had to explain to her why I said no, and if I change my mind, I'll have to be prepared to have a discussion whether I'm tired or not. The crying spells are real, but don't be manipulated when it comes to bedtime, schoolwork, and home chores/requirements. Don't let him/her use their situation as a crutch.

Rob and Abby Smith

Follow your "gut" feeling. Just don't take any child and hope it's going to work or try and make it work. Wait for that "feeling" that you just "KNOW" this one or ones are yours. The right ones just work.

Don't be disappointed and give up if your first match doesn't work. We declined two matches before we found our kids.

Be very specific on which issues a child may have that you feel like you can handle. If you don't think you can handle a child with fetal alcohol syndrome, say so. It's better to take a little longer and get the right match, for both you and the child.

Stay on top of your case yourself, just to the point of thinking you're being a nuisance. Ask your Social Worker if they'd rather you e-mailed them or called them and how often to check in. We learned by working WITH your Social Worker they will work harder for you. You have to know that they do get sidetracked with different emergencies.

The system isn't perfect and many mistakes are liable to happen. Case workers are overloaded and understaffed. Have patience.

Parenting Tips from Rob and Abby Smith

Don't "baby" them because they've had a hard time of it. Start from day one teaching them your house rules and holding them accountable.

Don't make a promise you can't keep and always, always, always follow through no matter what on anything you say whether it's positive or negative.

When you say "no" it means "no" and they have to understand that.

Never give up no matter how tough things are at that moment. It is always better to calm down, take a step back and look at the situation from another angle. That's when you will see the root of the issue and be able to resolve it. There is always an answer and always a way to improve, change and make things better.

No matter what, always, always, always tell your family how much you love them and that you will always be there for them.

From a
Child's Heart

Appendix B

From the Heart of Darnell

It hasn't been easy you know.

I was living in a small crowded apartment. They were drinking and using drugs right in front of me. My big brother was my hero, but he once tried to suffocate me. The social worker, he said he was my friend. He took me to a stranger's house and left me there. I cried. I wanted to go home. I looked forward to my visits with my grandma. One day we waited and waited, but in my heart I knew she wasn't coming. After a while, I gave up hope. I felt alone.

I was the little runt in most of my new foster homes. My foster brothers beat me up. I watched them get new parents and wondered why nobody came for me. I felt ugly and angry.

Imagine getting a box of Oreo cookies for Christmas while the other kids got toys. I cried. Imagine being told you have to go live somewhere else because you're too old. Imagine adoption fairs. But, that's when life changed!

I was adopted on my ninth birthday. I have real parents now. They took me out of all that junk. I had my first real Christmas with no Oreo cookies as Christmas gifts. I have my own bedroom and the kids at school. . . they actually like me! Especially the girls.

I know that I am loved. Mom says, "We see you as a shooting star, and you can do anything if you put your mind it."

Yeah . . . Life is better now.

Darnell

From the Heart of Austin

I knew everything there was to know about the foster system until someone spoke to me about adoption. The fact of me and my siblings being part of a loving family we can call Mom and Dad was overwhelming. It's been so long since my biological family last loved me and my siblings the way a loving family should, that's when I knew I wanted a family to call Mom and Dad. From that moment on I understood adoption and yes it was what my siblings and I wanted. At first we thought about it and yes at first it was scary but I knew one day something special would come out of it.

Growing up even before the adoption, my biological parent were never there for us, so the day came when we were forced to live out in the streets, pick food from the garbage just for us to eat and get by. I was determined to protect my siblings and ensure their safety by any means necessary and in doing so I took a fatherly role at just the age of five. As time went on and we were forced to be placed in the foster care system, I made it a priority to keep my siblings and I together. There came a time where we did get separated but as I mentioned I made it a priority to keep us together and in doing so, my determination brought us back together.

When we were living in foster homes as I mention we were constantly being abused, to ensure the safety of my siblings, I took all of their beatings for them just so I wouldn't see them hurt. This was my way of protecting them. As we were adopted, my mindset was still set as the fatherly role to ensure their safety and because of my mindset with my new loving family we clashed a lot. I wasn't ready to let my siblings go. It wasn't an easy journey but we made it.

I had to let go and let my parents be parents. I began to trust them and really in the end of it all, love is what kept us together. The bond that we share as a family is unimaginable and it can NEVER, EVER be broken no matter where life may take us.

I learned that life isn't all sunshine and rainbows; of course I found that out at a young age. It wasn't till I got to college that I was able to understand who I really was as a man so I guess you can say, I found myself. In doing so I made a pact with myself to attend every Wednesday's child event so that I can reach out to these kids in the foster care system who are hurting to share my story.

The most important advice I can give to parents wanting to adopt is to be patient with them. Most of these kids have experienced things they should never have to experience. Be understanding and don't be quick to judge them. Give them a chance, open your hearts to these kids, give them a chance to let their life story be heard, we all have one. Encourage them, tell them you love them every day, believe in them.

These kids who are seeking a permanent family to love are a gift from God. Take my story and share it with others, open your hearts to these beautiful children and love as if they were your own. There are so many kids in this world without families, without a permanent home that are in desperate need of love and guidance. Be that person who can change a child's life.

Austin

From the Heart of Madison

WOW! I Can't Believe It's Been Six Years!
An Essay by Madison

WOW! I can't believe it has been almost six years that I've been with my family.

My dad can't believe that I have grown so tall and the same with my mom. When I first came to my family I was only up to my mom and dad's hips, but now I'm up to his chin and her nose! WOW!! MIRACULOUS!!

Did you know that I have been moved eight times? I used to be a foster child, meaning I could not stay with my birth mom because she wasn't able to take care of me! Foster homes are not permanent homes, so I got moved eight times, and the seventh home I stayed in was not very pretty at all. The school I went to wasn't a very good one. WOW! What a difference it was switching to (school name)!

Six years ago this December I was my parents' Christmas present. WOW, did they love it! My uncle put a big red bow in my hair and I came out with a big smile on my face. My mom and dad were so happy.

For a while I was my mom's magnet. I never stopped following her around the house and I even went into the bathroom with her, but finally she told me to stay on the other side of the door.

A month later we went to see my brothers, Austin & Joey. They were in a different foster home than I was. When I was there we were so happy because we hadn't seen each other for six months. WOW!! That's a long time to be separated. One week later they moved into our home and we were finally together again! After a while, we were adopted.

WOW!! I can't believe that it has been six years that I've been with my brothers and my mom and dad and WOW we are a really happy family!

Madison

Appendix C

Resources

Christine's Corner—Books of Interest

Exactly As I Am by Shaun Robinson

Delivering Happiness by Tony Hsieh

Side By Side The Revolutionary Mother-Daughter Program for Conflict-Free Communication by Dr. Charles Sophy

The Women Who Raised Me byVictoria Rowell

Finding Fish by Antwone Fisher

Somebody's Someone by Regina Louise

Just Lucky I Guess by Carol Channing

Ten Things I Wish I'd Known by Maria Shriver

Just Who Will You Be by Maria Shriver

Powerful Inspirations by Kathy Ireland

The Purpose Driven Life by Rick Warren

How To Win Friends and Influence People by Dale Carnegie

Who Moved My Cheese by Spencer Johnson

The 7 Habits of Highly Effective People by Stephen R. Covey

People of the Lie by M. Scott Peck

Cinderella and Her Sister by Ann and Barry Ulanov

Finding a Man Worth Keeping by Victorya Michaels Rogers

Getting to I Do by Pat Allen

The Wounded Woman by Linda Schierse Leonard

The Ms. Money Book by Emily Card

Crunch Time by Ken Lindner

Power Plays by Robert Mayer

Confessions of a Prairie Bitch, How I Survived Nellie Oleson and Learned to Love Being Hated by Allison Arngrim

Co-dependent No More by Melody Beattie

Setting Boundaries with Your Adult Children, Six Steps to Hope and Healing for Struggling Parents by Allison Bottke

Will's Reads:

Adoption and Ethics, Volume 1: The Role of Race, Culture, and National Origin in Adoption by Madelyn Freundlich

Adoption and Ethics, Volume 3: The Impact of Adoption on Members of the Triad by Madelyn Freundlich

Adoption and Prenatal Alcohol & Drug Exposure: Research, Policy, and Practice by Richard Barth, Madelyn Freundlich, David Brodzinsky

Attachment, Trauma, and Healing: Understanding and Treating Attachment Disorder in Children and Families by Terry M. Levy, Michael Orlans

Lesbian and Gay Foster and Adoptive Parents: Recruiting, Assessing, and Supporting an Untapped Resource for Children and Youth by Gerald P. Mallon

Lifegivers: Framing the Birthparent Experience in Open Adoption by James L. Gritter

Making Cultural Connections: Hair and Skin Care for Children of African Descent by Jeanne M. Costa

Tender Mercies: Inside the World of a Child Abuse Investigator by Keith N. Richards

The Postadoption Experience: Adoptive Families' Service Needs and Service Outcomes—Casey Family Services Publication

The Spirit of Open Adoption by James L. Gritter

Transracial Adoption and Foster Care: Practice Issues for Professionals by Joseph Crumbley

Working with Traumatized Children: A Handbook for Healing Revised Edition by Kathryn Brohl

Will's Resources

General adoption information
http://www.yougottabelieve.org
(Adopting Older Kids And Youth is A-OKAY)

Adopting.com
http://www.adopting.com
Resources for prospective adoptive parents

Adopting.org
http://www.adopting.org
Contains a wide variety of adoption topics and resources.

Adoption Information
http://adoption.about.com
Articles and tips for those considering adoption and for those who have adopted.

Adoption.com
http://www.adoption.com
Contains a wide variety of adoption topics and resources.

Adoption.org
http://www.adoption.org
Contains a wide variety of adoption topics and resources.

Adoptive Families Magazine
http://www.adoptivefamilies.com
Publication focusing on adoptive and prospective adoptive families.

Foster Family to Forever Family
http://www.adopt.org/assembled/overview_courses.html
The first course in "The Adoption Roadmap" online training series.

North American Council on Adoptable Children
http://www.nacac.org
General information on how each state operates their Title IV-E Adoption Assistance program.

Foster Care Adoption

Adopt America Network
http://www.adoptamericanetwork.org
Adopt America Network places special needs children into permanent homes.

Adopt US Kids
http://www.adoptuskids.org
This site, launched in 2002, is funded by the U.S. government.

Child Welfare Information Gateway
http://www.childwelfare.gov
A comprehensive resource on all aspects of adoption.
National Adoption Directory.

Fostering Connections Resource Center
http://www.fosteringconnections.org
An online resource center for furthering the implementation of the Fostering Connections law.
Kidsave.org
http://www.kidsave.org
Kidsave works to help older orphaned and abandoned children find families.

Adoption Benefits

Adoption Policy Resource Center
http://www.fpsol.com/adoption/advocates.html
Free initial consultation and related policy information.

National Center for Adoption Law and Policy
http://www.law.capital.edu/adoption
Seeks to improve the law, policies and practices associated with child protection and adoption systems.

Financial Assistance

Bank of America
http://www.bankofamerica.com
Bank of America offers unsecured loans specifically designed for adoptive parents.

Gift of Adoption Fund
http://www.giftofadoption.org
Helps families overcome some of the initial financial burdens of adoption (home study, legal fees, etc.).

HelpUsAdopt.org
http://www.helpusadopt.org
Will provide qualified couples and individuals (regardless of race, religion, marital status or sexual preference) with grants.

Show Hope (Shaohannah's Hope)
http://www.showhope.org
Awards financial grants to qualified families already in the process of domestic and international adoption.

The National Adoption Foundation
http://www.nafadopt.org
Offers an Adoption Assistance Loan.

The Orphan Foundation
http://www.TheOrphanFoundation.org
Providing grants of $1,000 for each child adopted, and $1,500 for each "special needs" adoption.

WACAP—World Association for Children and Parents
http://www.wacap.org
Special funds and programs to help parents cover the costs of certain adoptions.

Exchanges and Photolistings

Adoptable Kids
http://www.adoptablekids.com
Photolisting of children awaiting adoption.

Jewish Children's Adoption Network
http://jcan.qwestoffice.net
The only Jewish adoption exchange in the Western hemisphere.

The Adoption Exchange
http://www.adoptex.org
Provides the connection between families who adopt and children who wait and is a place for the exchange of resources on behalf of dozens of adoption agencies.

Policy and Legislation

Adoption Policy Resource Center
http://www.fpsol.com/adoption/advocates.html
Provides free initial consultation and related policy information.

All Children—All Families Initiative
http://www.hrc.org/issues/8399.htm
An initiative of the Human Rights Campaign to educate and engage the gay, lesbian, bisexual and transgender (GLBT) community in foster and adoptive parenting.

American Bar Association Center on Children and the Law
http://www.abanet.org/child
The Center is a full-service technical assistance, training, and research program addressing a broad spectrum of law and court-related topics.

Child Welfare League of America
http://www.cwla.org
Promotes the well-being of children, youth, and their families, and is committed to protecting every child from harm.

Congressional Coalition on Adoption Institute
http://www.ccainstitute.org

A nonprofit, nonpartisan organization dedicated to raising Congressional and public awareness.

Evan B. Donaldson Adoption Institute
http://www.adoptioninstitute.org
Provides adoption information to media, lawmakers and individuals on topics such as survey data and governmental research data.

Fostering Connections Resource Center
http://www.fosteringconnections.org
An online resource center with information, training and tools for furthering the implementation of the Fostering Connections law.

Human Rights Campaign
http://www.hrc.org/issues/parenting/adoption.asp
Offers adoption resources and advocacy for gay, lesbian bisexual and transgender parents.

Joint Council on International Children Services
http://www.jcics.org
JCICS is a membership organization which advocates on behalf of parentless children worldwide.

National Center for Adoption Law and Policy
http://www.law.capital.edu/adoption
Seeks to improve the law, policies and practices associated with child protection and adoption systems.

State Child Welfare Policy Database
http://www.childwelfarepolicy.org/pages/map.cfm
Child Trends, with support from Casey Family Programs, hosts a website that acts as the clearinghouse for state child welfare policies.

Acknowledgements

Thanks Mom for showing me we all have something to offer in our very own way, at our very own time, in our very own place. In telling my story, you allowed me to tell yours. Words cannot express my gratitude for your openness and answers.

To my beautiful blonde baby sister Danielle, "you could have been a therapist" I lecture. Unofficially, you were. Thank you "Digny" for being my rock. It is a role a baby sister shouldn't have to play and I am forever grateful. We'll always be "Mr. Green" and "Mrs. Bli-bi-bla." A shout out to your hubby, Lance. Thanks for showing me what a husband should look like. To baby-girl Skylar... I'm saving all my designer gowns for you. We will play dress up for the rest of our lives!

To Sean McNabb, the man I'm going to marry. "Where have you been all my life???" You ROCK, literally! Thank you for loving Christine Devine and "Chrissy."

To my late grandparents Dolores and Julius Seufert, North Boston, New York will forever be my paradise! To my late father, Jack Devine... you took me in as your own. Nothing but respect! To my foster sister Bao Tran Nguyen, soul-sisters from day one. I love ya so much!!!

You can't be YOU without a team. To my agent Ken Lindner: Thank you for your vision! Much love to Shari Freis and Karen Wang. To my attorney and mentor Emily Card who would hound me with this question, "Why don't you write a book?" Thank you for planting the seed. To Dr. Pat Allen who wrote *Getting to I Do*. I am! To Bennett Williamson, my voice of sanity. Thanks for the free therapy while getting your Ph.D. in psychology. Oh, did you graduate years ago? And I'm still calling for free therapy? Sorry! To Paulara Hawkins. I only see you as this: Skilled screenwriter, author, playwright. The world awaits you!

Being single for MANY, MANY years you can't help but have "your girls"... Cristina Coria, Rana Schirmer, Wendy Burch, "cousin" Kyona Beatty, Angelina Kwong, Jennifer Gould Therese Bisignano and new gal-pal Leslie Seigel. Thanks Angie Austin for the early L.A. days. Thanks Amy Waddell for letting me crash on your couch. Thanks Carolyn Pendergast for the Tolleson High Camero car rides and Lupe Rivera for the laughter. Go Wolverines! To Todd Davis, you'll so get the "Mike" stories. And I still "don't want anyone to recognize me." Hee hee!

To Arizona State University, guess my journalism degree from the Walter Cronkite school has gone to good use. Thank you Christine Wilkinson for selecting me for Leadership Scholarship in high school, sealing the deal. To professor Ben Silver, thanks for taking my college resume and posting it on the bulletin board at a news director's convention. I got the job! A shout out to Eddie Devall, ASU's Cali connection. To college roomies Kym, Patty & Webber, love from L.A. Thanks to Tolleson High Journalism instructor Mr. Cooper who lectured me once "Ya know Christine, there's more to life than cheerleading." To my Tolleson High teachers, was so nice to know you. Thanks to News Directors Arthur Wood and Brink Chipman and for my first on-air jobs.

To the Good News Foundation girls. They can never again say "the news is all negative." Love my Good News Girls: Wendy Burch, Pat Harvey, Dorothy Lucey and Ana Garcia.

To TEAM WC... that's anyone who's ever been involved with Wednesday's Child. On the Fox 11 side that includes KTTV General Manager Kevin Hale and Vice President/News Director Jose Rios. Jose launched the effort fifteen years ago and never let it go. Jose, thanks for allowing me to be your anchor for all these years. Humbled and honored!

Thanks to ALL at Fox for your enthusiasm and energy. To my TEAM WC colleagues, Veronica Carrillo in Fox Sales and Caroline Janik Wong in Creative Services... Wednesday's Child is your baby too! To Yolanda Santana, you are a graphics goddess. Thanks to the editors and photographers, can't do the segment without ya! To Assignment Manager Carol Breshears, will you adopt me??? Thanks for your input on the book. To Gene O'Neill my work-papa. No, I still won't quit my job if we win the lottery, but get me a ticket anyway! Thanks for lugging all my notes to the car and back. To Abe Rosenberg, thank you for your wisdom on WC. To Jerry Cash and Danielle Fortier, hair and makeup AND free counseling??? Know our talks got me to this point, Miss ya. To John Beard, Rick Garcia and Mark Thompson, love ya! Luv to my first colleagues Jane Yamamoto, Jeff Michael, Greg Montemurro and Al Naipo.

TEAM WC includes EVERY SINGLE social worker on the planet, for YOU are doin' the unsung hard work. In L.A. County thank you to former DCFS Director Trish Ploehn and your executive staff (Joi, Bill, Diane, Sari, Brian, Amy, Estelle, Nick, Neil and former Sunday's Child Coordinator Wendy Tashiro). To Social Worker, Will Wong, my WC "husband," this book is OUR book! And Agnes loves ya. Thanks Naehi for sharing Will and allowing me to steal precious at home time. Yes, Will, we can ask actor Jack Black to play you in the movie!

To the Freddie Mac Foundation, you brought life to this issue in Los Angeles. Foundation C.E.O. Ralph Boyd FOR PRESIDENT! Renette Oklewicz, we always aimed to make YOU proud. Props to NBC4 Anchorwoman Barbara Harrison of D.C. who brought the idea to the Freddie Mac Foundation launching this national effort.

To our adoptive families. You light up my life! To the kids in the book, a great big hug! I applaud your strength and honor your candor. To all the children ever on our segment, you are my babies! To Maureen Thomas, you are superwoman!

Finally, to the viewers of Fox 11 News. I can't do it without ya. The fact that you tune in to watch li'l ol' me continues to leave me awe-struck! To every national network news outlet that never came calling, thank you! It allowed me more than fifteen years with Wednesday's Child. It allowed me "such a time as this."

To Stacia Oemig, and Project Nightlight, thank you for your continued partnership. Thank God for you and your work "empowering teens to overcome abuse"!

To all those who gave me such wonderful endorsements. You are my teachers!

To Michael Herbach, you take a mean headshot! Thanks for the book cover photo and all others over the years.

To my INCREDIBLE editor Allison Bottke. You turned my notebook, my jumbled mess of notes and loose chapters, into a real-life book, and did it under an extreme deadline. Impressed and in appreciation. God bless!

And to author, agent, wife, mother, and friend Victorya Michaels Rogers. You continue to be my role model woman in every way. "Are we still walking?"

As it is not promised I'll write another book I took this time to thank many, knowing there are many more so worthy of mention. Know I send my appreciation and prayers.

About The Author

Christine Devine

Christine Devine resides in Los Angeles, California. She is a television news anchor, reporter, producer... and philanthropist. She has written and produced award-winning half-hour specials on adoption, Avon's walk to fight breast cancer, and Habitat for Humanity.

In L.A. Christine is recognized for her televised adoption segment, the Freddie Mac Foundation's Wednesday's Child for which she was honored by the Child Welfare League of America. Since 1994 she has profiled hard-to-place children in foster care waiting to be adopted. More than 500 children have found forever homes.

She is the recipient of numerous awards and honors, including:

14 Emmys

Best Anchor Team by Associated Press

Gracie Allen award, AWRT American Women in Radio and Television

Anna Quindlen award for philanthropy journalism, Society of Professional Journalists

Angels in Adoption—CCAI Congressional Coalition on Adoption Institute

Media Volunteer of the Year by Volunteers of America (L.A.)

An alumna of Arizona State University, Christine is in the Hall of Fame at the Walter Cronkite School of Broadcast Journalism. Christine is on ASU's National Alumni Council, has received the Young Alumni Achievement award and was also a recipient of the Medallion of Merit and Leadership Scholarship. She has also funded her own journalism scholarship.

Christine is a co-founder of The Good News Foundation, a non-profit organization built by five TV newswomen dedicated to honoring good news and good works in Los Angeles. GNF awards scholarships, grants and sponsors the annual "Legacy Project" designed to leave a lasting impact on the community. GNF was honored with the "Inspiration Award" by AWRT American Women in Radio and Television.

An active community supporter, Christine has been honored before the L.A. City Council, L.A. County Board of Supervisors, and by the Los Angeles Police Department and L.A. County Sheriff's Department. In 2007, LAPD's Hollenbeck division named her "Humanitarian of the Year."

In Hollywood, she has played a reporter on TV and in film, including *Melrose Place*, *90210*, *24*, *Wag the Dog*, *Independence Day*, *Cable Guy*, and *Most Wanted.*

Christine anchors the weeknight newscast on KTTV Fox 11 10 p.m. and sister-station KCOP Channel 13 11 p.m. news.

She is from upstate New York, but grew up in Arizona. Her parents adopted one boy and fostered a total five children from Vietnam. For more information on Christine Devine, or to book her as a speaker for your event, visit ChristineDevine.com

About the Editor

Allison Bottke

Allison Bottke is a bestselling inspirational author and speaker. Her international outreach includes over twenty-five published non-fiction and fiction books, including the acclaimed *God Allows U-Turns* compilation book series, the *God Answers Prayers* series, and the new *Setting Boundaries* series.

A frequent guest on national radio and TV programs, she has been featured on *James Dobson's Focus on the Family,* the *Dr. Laura Show, Decision Today,* and others. Allison is a frequent studio guest on *Good Morning Texas*.

Her book, *Setting Boundaries with Your Adult Children* is being heralded as a landmark resource for parents and grandparents and has hit #1 on the Amazon.com parenting list several times. *Setting Boundaries with Your Aging Parents* was released in 2009, and the third book in the series, *Setting Boundaries with Difficult People* will release in 2011, all are published by Harvest House Publishers.

She's published in *Writer's Digest*, *Ladies Home Journal*, *Cosmopolitan*, *Women's World*, and more. Allison has been on faculty at several national writing conferences, including Jerry B. Jenkins Writing for the Soul, and the North Texas Christian Writers Conference. Allison has a passion to help writers make their publishing dreams come true. She owns a private consulting business and lives in Fort Worth, Texas. Visit: AllisonBottke.com

Intermedia
Publishing Group
Publishing That Works For You

Whether you want to purchase bulk copies of *Finding a Forever Family* or buy another book for a friend, get it now at: imprbooks.com.

If you have a book that you would like to publish, contact Terry Whalin, Publisher, at Intermedia Publishing Group, (623) 337-8710 or email: twhalin@intermediapub.com or use the contact form at: intermediapub.com.